Praise for Women of Strength

Women of Strength uniquely captures Dr. Thomas' heart concerning every woman's deepest, most intimate desire – to know, trust, and live for her heavenly Father. She identifies six key areas in which women should strive to develop themselves to satisfy their yearning for true intimacy with a loving God. She also presents biblical principles, which, when applied practically, will produce lasting results. When times are tough, women of faith stand strong. We don't give up. We don't make excuses. We don't run away from challenges. Instead, we simply trust God, lean on His promises and do whatever it takes to overcome and win's life's battles! Dr. Thomas has given us many wonderful examples of how to do just that through *Women of Strength*.

Taffi L. Dollar,
Pastor
World Changers Church
College Park, GA

How does one blend carefully chosen scriptures, family recipes, personal struggles and testimonies, and delightful stories of real people into one book? Very well, if you are Dr. Kiki Thomas! *Women of Strength* is full of encouragement, comfort, wisdom, confession, insight, reflection, honesty, and truth. As I read, I was drawn into Kiki's world of faith and family. I felt as if we were talking together in a quiet place and Kiki was leading me to a deeper trust in God alone. Was she a deeply committed disciple of Jesus Christ, a warm storyteller, a humble and penitent sinner who gladly pointed others to the Source of forgiveness, or sensitive counselor? All of those and more – to the glory of God alone.

Dr. Dennis E. Glenn,
Vice President for Academic Affairs
Atlanta Christian College
East Point, GA

This book is based on faith and trust in God. If you are looking for direction in your life, Women of *Strength: Six Promises to God*, can serve as a road map for you. In sharing her personal experiences and six promises to God. Dr. Kiki Thomas has opened her heart and made a noteworthy contribution to Christian literature. We pray that this book will touch the lives of many and help the women who don't know where to turn, but can find comfort in reading this book. Much love and well wishes for *Women of Strength*'s success are our hearts' desire.

Clarence and Shirley Cooper
Atlanta, GA

There are so many qualities that make women special. Perhaps one of the most admirable of these qualities is her strength. In *Women of Strength: Six Promises to God*, Dr. Kiki Thomas illuminates the power of such strength by intimately sharing personal experiences and also sharing how the Word of God proved to be a pillar of strength for her. The stories and scriptures she shares are moving – there are times of laughter and times of tears – all of which have a unique way of pushing one closer to God. I see reading *Women of Strength* as an opportunity to read, reflect, and rejoice! Thank you, Dr. Kiki, for sharing your heart and encouraging ours.

Alonia Jones
Principal, Dream 2 Destiny Enterprises
Servant Leader/Pastor
Dream to Destiny Ministries
East Point, GA

Women OF STRENGTH

SIX PROMISES TO GOD

Dr. Kiki Thomas

WESTBOW
PRESS®
A DIVISION OF THOMAS NELSON
& ZONDERVAN

WestBow Press books may be ordered through booksellers or by contacting:

WestBow Press
A Division of Thomas Nelson & Zondervan
1663 Liberty Drive
Bloomington, IN 47403
www.westbowpress.com
1 (866) 928-1240

Unless otherwise noted, all scripture is taken from
the King James Version of the Bible.

ISBN: 978-1-9736-2511-7 (sc)

Print information available on the last page.

WestBow Press rev. date: 5/31/2018

Contents

Acknowledgements

There are a number of special people whose names need to appear in big bold colors on these pages since this book would not have come to fruition without them. This book is dedicated to those Elect Women who have gone before us, and those who are still with us, who have consistently demonstrated the qualities of strength and faith even in the face of extreme difficulties. They have become my witnesses. Let us run the race as well as these Elect Women.

To Adleane (Granny, Mommy),
Darlene (Great-Aunt),
Stella (great woman of strength who reared my
Granny Adleane, Great-great-aunt),
Mary (my mom),
and Betty (Nanna, Beth, Aunt) who taught me about Jesus.

To my mom, Rose Mary:
What an awesome woman you are! I thank God
for you daily. You make this journey so
beautiful for Tony, Kiantki and me. Thank you
for standing in the gap and for all those
prayers you sent up for us.

To my Sweet Tony:
Thanks for your support, for your unfailing
strength, and for your unconditional love.
I love you!

To my only son, Kiantki:
Kiantki, my heart's jewel. You are all good inside and outside. I count it all JOY to be your mom. The lessons you have taught us will endure for generations to come. I love you so much.
Love, Mom.

To my sisters, Cookie and Wanda:
My prayer partners who love the Lord Jesus Christ. You are two of the sweetest women in this big wide world. I thank God for both of you. I remember you when I pray with joy, being confident of this, that he who began a good work in you will carry it on to completion until the day of Christ Jesus (Philippians 1:6).

To Marti Loring:
My true friend, Marti, who is strong and faith-filled always. Thank you, Marti, for your passion, support and talent. All you do is greatly appreciated.

To WestBow Press:
Thank you for all your support and enthusiasm. Thank you for awesome teamwork.

With all the people's names mentioned here, there are so many others I love who are not listed. I know you know me well, and you know that you are in my heart. What a special group you are!

And now to my Lord and Savior,
who can do exceedingly, abundantly more than we could ever ask or think in Christ Jesus: I pray, Lord Jesus, that my life is expressed as a thank you to you for all you have done in my life. I am and always will be yours.

With all of my love and affection, KT.

Introduction

Life is simply too hard to face alone. After having faced my share of life's ups and downs, highs and lows, goods and bads, joys and pains, as well as days of laughter and days of sorrow, that is the conclusion to which I have come. Indeed, I am convinced that without faith in God, the journey would be much more tedious. This reminds me of the words to a Gospel classic that was first recorded by the Gospel legend, Mahalia Jackson. In later years, it was recorded again by Ricky Dillard and the New Generation Choir. The name of the song is, "Without God," and some of its lyrics say:

> *Without a doubt, he is my Savior,*
> *Yes, my strength, along life's waves.*
> *Yes, in deep waters, my God, he is my anchor.*
> *Lord, and through faith he'll keep me always.*
> *Without God, I could do nothing.*
> *Without him, I would fail.*
> *Without God, my life would be rugged.*
> *Like a ship without a sail.*

So here I am: a witness to the goodness of God and his wonder-working power! I believe God has placed many gifts in my hands. One in particular is the ability to minister to women. I want you to know that the gift of ministering is not exclusive to those who mount a pulpit every day of worship. No, it is not only for those who bear the title of Reverend or Minister or Pastor. Yes, Ephesians 4:11 tells us that there is the fivefold ministry of apostles, prophets, evangelists, pastors, and teachers. Nevertheless, according to 1 Corinthians 4:1, servants of God are also his ambassadors. As such, we have a responsibility to minister to whomever he directs us: "Let a man so account of us, as of the ministers of Christ, and stewards of the mysteries of God" (1 Corinthians 4:1). With this joyful revelation in mind, it is my honor that the fruit of my labor has undoubtedly identified my audience to which to minister is women.

In preparing this literary work, I have thought and prayed long and hard. I wanted to share from the depths of my soul six promises that will help women's walk with God become stronger. To that end, my hope is that this book will help other women hear God's voice more clearly. I pray that somehow these testimonies will encourage women everywhere to connect with the Lord, turning to him in faith always and not giving in to what the enemy brings them. I pray also that God will empower these pages to remind you of how very much he loves you.

Furthermore, my purpose in writing this book and many more is that some woman somewhere will pick it up and hear God's word like she's never heard before. Or perhaps she has forgotten him. Then my prayer is that these pages will touch her heart, help her to hear more closely and feel more completely the word from the lips of our Lord and Savior Jesus Christ who adores her. His love for his daughters is immense and real.

Sincerely,
Dr. Kiki Thomas

Promise One

TO HAVE FAITH IN YOU, DEAR GOD, EVEN WHEN I CANNOT SEE YOU

Faith means believing what I am hoping for. That is what the Bible tells us in Hebrews 11:1, "Now faith is the substance of things hoped for, the evidence of things not seen." In other words, it takes faith to believe beyond what we see and to have belief in the God whom we expect to see when life is over on earth. People who are unbelievers practice faith, although they probably do not realize they are doing so. But if we, as believers, place our faith in things other than God, we cannot please him. We must use our faith to believe that God is right here with us every moment—right now and always!

Perhaps there are those who are wondering how it is even possible for believers to use our faith to believe God is with us and working on our behalf while on earth, let alone when this life is over. After all, if we were to be completely honest with ourselves, life is sure to present a number of challenges. The book of Job tells us is in chapter 14 and verse 1 that man that's born of a woman is of few days, and those days are full of trouble. The Bible further tells us in Matthew

5:45 that God makes the sun rise on the evil and on the good, and that he sends rain on the just and on the unjust.

As a result, many people have found themselves being tossed and turned, and being like that ship without a sail that I referenced in the Introduction. I know for a fact that some odds of life are seemingly insurmountable. For example, take a moment to think about how many people you know who are facing or have faced one of the following situations:

- One or more health crises
- Wayward children
- Infidelity
- Rape
- Betrayal by so-called friends
- Addictions
- Poverty
- Lack of education
- Aging parents
- Mental health challenges
- Unjustifiable wrongs that have been committed against you
- Racism
- Divorce

Without question, this list could go on and on. But as I mention these situations, please know that I am not speaking of them in general terms. Instead, what I am hoping you will see is that each of these circumstances can be extreme. Allow me to expound on these random examples for a brief moment:

- That health crisis can be in the form of an incurable disease that has plagued one who has previously been in perfectly good health all of his/her life.

- Wayward children could be an unexplainable result to parents who have done all they could to bring their children up in the "right way."
- Infidelity could happen to the most undeserving spouse ever.
- Rape is never an invited action. Who asks for that?
- The betrayal of so-called friends leaves an indelible mark that can never be forgotten and can cause barriers to trust that will last forever.
- Addictions, like trouble, can be easy to come to us but difficult to get off us, if at all.
- Poverty could seem to be an inescapable stronghold that has plagued people for generation.
- When there is a lack of education, people are limited in many areas of life, which could further perpetuate the plague of poverty. It can also contribute to the lack of self-esteem and so many other security boosters.
- The reality of caring for aging parents is a culture shock for many people. It is enough to try to take care of one's self. To face the reality of having to see about the well-being of those who have once taken care of you (or not, in some instances) can be more than a notion.
- Although it has long been a taboo topic (particularly in the African American community), mental health is a real problem. However, because too few conversations about it have taken place, its' by products create more challenges than many would like to admit.
- When people treat you wrong for no justifiable reason, it can create a pain beyond description. To say that this is painful is an understatement.
- Racism has a long history of having an adverse impact on society. The journey to eradicate it is never-ending, yet the battle is rather painstaking, to say the least.
- And as it relates to divorce, who willingly gets married only to get divorced? Of course, there are those who have ulterior

motives. But for the most part, most decent people marry with the hopes of spending the rest of their lives with the one to whom they made such a vow. When the marriage is dissolved, it could be devastating.

Again, this list could go on and on. I expounded on these circumstances to remind you that faith can certainly be something that is difficult to find in the midst of extreme circumstances. Undoubtedly, you will find yourself asking, "How can I have faith when I can't even see God in the midst of what is happening to me in this situation. Where is he anyway?"

Although it is difficult, it is not impossible. What I have discovered in my lifetime is that faith is not something that we are inherently born with. Instead, faith is something that must be built. The Bible teaches in Romans 10:17 that faith comes by hearing, and the hearing that we need is through the Word of God.

As we hear the Word of God and allow it to penetrate our spirit, it will help us to trust that God will see us through any and every situation that we may face. The songwriter put it this way:

> 'Tis so sweet to trust in Jesus.
> Just to take him at his word.
> Just to rest upon his promise.
> Just to know, "Thus saith the Lord!"
> Jesus, Jesus. How I trust him.
> How I've proved him o'er and o'er.
> Jesus, Jesus. Precious Jesus.
> O, for grace to trust him more.

Is this to say that we should not face the fact that life can be hard and that situations can bring tears to our eyes? Absolutely not! What we can say is that, because of our faith, we have hope that things will eventually get better. And even if they don't or if things don't work out in our best interest or how we would so desire them to, our faith tells us that, regardless of the circumstances, God is working everything out for his children's good: "And we know that all things work together for good to them that love God, to them who are the called according to his purpose" (Romans 8:28).

The key word in that verse is *know.* You see, when you have a personal relationship with Jesus Christ, when you have accepted him as your personal lord and savior, there are some things you will simply know. You will be confident that he will see you through whatever you are going through. In so knowing, you will find yourself having the courage to withstand the fiery trials of life. That is what faith is all about: trusting God even when you cannot see him. There will be something on the inside of you encouraging you to hold on, pray on, press on just a little while longer. I am a witness: if you totally put your trust in God, he will give you everything you need to trust him even when you cannot see him.

Promise Two

TO ENCOURAGE OTHERS TO HAVE FAITH IN YOU, DEAR LORD

We must use our faith to believe that God exists, because without faith it is impossible to please God. Anyone who comes to him must believe that he exists and that he rewards those who earnestly seek him (Hebrews 11:6).

Faith. What does it mean? Those who wait on the Lord will find new strength. They will fly high on wings like eagles. They will run and not grow weary. They will walk and not faint (Isaiah 40:31). We all have a lot of activity going on in our lives. Naturally, we are curious about the future. We often worry a great deal about the directions the Lord will provide for us. However, we must not allow fear to take over. We have to rely on faith in these areas of our lives. I am not speaking of the kind of faith that involves whether we believe in Jesus. Neither am I speaking of faith about whether we stay committed to him. Rather, I am speaking of the kind of faith that trusts God in spite of the trials we face.

I encourage you to have this deep and abiding faith in our Lord. With all the worldly encouragement we offer to others, why is it so rare to encourage faith in God? I want to encourage your faith to flourish and deepen.

You can trust God's timing. You can trust his guidance and direction for your life. Having faith in God is more than just being sure of his existence. It is a way of giving all control of your life to Jesus Christ. Real faith means you can relax and know that God will do what his promises say he will do. Hebrews 11 says:

> Now faith is the substance of things hoped for, the evidence of things not seen. For by it the elders obtained a good report. Through faith we understand that the worlds were framed by the word of God, so that things which are seen were not made of things which do appear.
>
> By faith Abel offered unto God a more excellent sacrifice than Cain, by which he obtained witness that he was righteous, God testifying of his gifts: and by it he being dead yet speaketh.
>
> By faith Enoch was translated that he should not see death; and was not found, because God had translated him: for before his translation he had this testimony, that he pleased God. But without faith it is impossible to please him: for he that cometh to God must believe that he is, and that he is a rewarder of them that diligently seek him.
>
> By faith Noah, being warned of God of things not seen as yet, moved with fear, prepared an ark to the saving of his house; by the which he condemned the

world, and became heir of the righteousness which is by faith.

By faith Abraham, when he was called to go out into a place which he should after receive for an inheritance, obeyed; and he went out, not knowing whither he went.

By faith he sojourned in the land of promise, as in a strange country, dwelling in tabernacles with Isaac and Jacob, the heirs with him of the same promise: For he looked for a city which hath foundations, whose builder and maker is God.

Through faith also Sara herself received strength to conceive seed, and was delivered of a child when she was past age, because she judged him faithful who had promised. Therefore sprang there even of one, and him as good as dead, so many as the stars of the sky in multitude, and as the sand which is by the sea shore innumerable. These all died in faith, not having received the promises, but having seen them afar off, and were persuaded of them, and embraced them, and confessed that they were strangers and pilgrims on the earth. For they that say such things declare plainly that they seek a country. And truly, if they had been mindful of that country from whence they came out, they might have had opportunity to have returned. But now they desire a better country, that is, an heavenly: wherefore God is not ashamed to be called their God: for he hath prepared for them a city.

By faith Abraham, when he was tried, offered up Isaac: and he that had received the promises offered up his only begotten son, Of whom it was said, That in Isaac shall thy seed be called: Accounting that God was able to raise him up, even from the dead; from whence also he received him in a figure.

By faith Isaac blessed Jacob and Esau concerning things to come.

By faith Jacob, when he was a dying, blessed both the sons of Joseph; and worshipped, leaning upon the top of his staff.

By faith Joseph, when he died, made mention of the departing of the children of Israel; and gave commandment concerning his bones.

By faith Moses, when he was born, was hid three months of his parents, because they saw he was a proper child; and they were not afraid of the king's commandment

By faith Moses, when he was come to years, refused to be called the son of Pharaoh's daughter; Choosing rather to suffer affliction with the people of God, than to enjoy the pleasures of sin for a season; Esteeming the reproach of Christ greater riches than the treasures in Egypt: for he had respect unto the recompence of the reward.

By faith he forsook Egypt, not fearing the wrath of the king: for he endured, as seeing him who is invisible. Through faith he kept the passover, and the sprinkling of blood, lest he that destroyed the firstborn should touch them.

By faith they passed through the Red sea as by dry land: which the Egyptians assaying to do were drowned. By faith the walls of Jericho fell down, after they were compassed about seven days. By faith the harlot Rahab perished not with them that believed not, when she had received the spies with peace.

And what shall I more say? for the time would fail me to tell of Gedeon, and of Barak, and of Samson, and of Jephthae; of David also, and Samuel, and of the prophets: Who through faith subdued kingdoms, wrought righteousness, obtained promises, stopped the mouths of lions, Quenched the violence of fire, escaped the edge of the sword, out of weakness were made strong, waxed valiant in fight, turned to flight the armies of the aliens. Women received their dead raised to life again: and others were tortured, not accepting deliverance; that they might obtain a better resurrection:

And others had trial of cruel mockings and scourgings, yea, moreover of bonds and imprisonment: They were stoned, they were sawn asunder, were tempted, were slain with the sword: they wandered about in sheepskins and goatskins; being destitute, afflicted, tormented; (Of whom the world was not worthy:) they wandered in deserts, and in mountains, and in dens and caves of the earth. And these all, having obtained a good report through faith, received not the promise: God having provided some better thing for us, that they without us should not be made perfect.

Our faith needs to grow until we can trust Almighty God with everything. Then we can pray as Christ did on the night before his crucifixion: "Father all things are possible for you" (Mark 14:36).

When we truly trust God, we can stand in times of trouble—just like the three Hebrew men who loved God. These three men were so faithful to him that when King Nebuchadnezzar ordered them to bow down to his golden image or be thrown into the fiery furnace, they refused. This is what they said to the king. Daniel 3:17–18 says:

> If it be so, our God whom we serve is able to deliver us from the burning fiery furnace, and he will deliver us out of thine hand, O king. But if not, be it known unto thee, O king, that we will not serve thy gods, nor worship the golden image which thou hast set up.

These men exercised their faith, but they surrendered to the will of Almighty God. Our faith will never override the will of God. There are times when it's God's will that we protest, as did faithful Jacob when he wrestled with the angel.

We can say faith is the key to stability and the cornerstone of life.
Life is tough. Faith will get you through.
When God is with us, who can be against us?
Never compromise your character to achieve any goal.
Faith takes courage and is rewarded.
Faith is everlasting.

I encourage you to grow in faith now and always. Make it your promise to God.

The Lord wants us to learn to trust him now and forever. That is what real faith is. We should not become too anxious to know what God's plans are.

> "For I know the thoughts that I think toward you, saith the LORD, thoughts of peace, and not of evil, to give you an expected end" (Jeremiah 29:11).

He will surely allow you the opportunity to know him and to learn his timing, what he has for you, and what he will give to you. Just keep the faith. It's so simple. All you have to do is allow God to be God and be in charge—always. Remember the story of Daniel in the lion's den? God wants the glory—always. God must receive the glory. God is God. He doesn't need help from us.

Ask God to deliver you from the evil one. Cry out to God. Ask him to deliver you from whatever you are experiencing that is not of him. When God blesses you, the devil will want you to think it's you.

No, it's God and he gets the glory.

Stay focused and give God all the GLORY!

Let God be God.

Here are additional scriptures to help with your faith. Faith listens and responds.

Romans 10:17 says, "So then faith cometh by hearing, and hearing by the word of God." This verse helps us recognize the relationship between faith and hearing the Word of God. Be determined to stay sensitive to God's call through the reading of his Word and through prayer.

The story of Samuel is an excellent example. Samuel had to listen very carefully in order to hear God. It takes a keen sense of listening to hear what God is saying. When you pray, ask God to help you hear his voice.

In other words, Samuel was prepared to hear God. He had spent years and years in the temple studying God's Word and preparing his heart for service. God knew Samuel had a willing heart. He knew that Samuel was waiting on his call.

If we make a point to be open to God and to draw closer to him each day, God will speak to us. He will guide us the same way that he did Samuel--not by speaking out loud, but we will hear him just the same.

What are you doing now to prepare yourself for God's call?

Faith means that I trust God, though I know it doesn't mean that everything is going to be easy. We all know life is tough, and we all have to be tough, too. Each day we live, there will be stuff to deal with. As children of the Lord Jesus, we don't know what tomorrow holds, but we do know who holds tomorrow. God makes all things possible to those who believe. Get to know him. He will bless you more than you can imagine.

> "And all things, whatsoever ye shall ask in prayer, believing, ye shall receive" (Matthew 21:22).
>
> "Jesus said unto him, If thou canst believe, all things are possible to him that believeth" (Mark 9:23).
>
> "And the Lord said, If ye had faith as a grain of mustard seed, ye might say unto this sycamine tree, Be thou plucked up by the root, and be thou planted in the sea; and it should obey you" (Luke 17:6).
>
> "Therefore I say unto you, What things soever ye desire, when ye pray, believe that ye receive them, and ye shall have them" (Mark 11:24).
>
> "He staggered not at the promise of God through unbelief; but was strong in faith, giving glory to God; And being fully persuaded that, what he had promised, he was able also to perform" (Romans 4:20, 21).

"Above all, taking the shield of faith, wherewith ye shall be able to quench all the fiery darts of the wicked" (Ephesians 6:16).

Faith. It's all about allowing Jesus Christ to take complete control of your life, complete charge of all, everything you could ever dream or think.

I encourage you to allow him to guide you in every way.

We may not be as indispensable as we think, but we are more beloved than we ever dreamed of. God looks for those of us whose hearts are fully sold out to him. And when he finds us—as he always does—he strengthens us.

Let us remember it is not about us and not up to us. Remember God's faithfulness, trust, mercy and grace. Our salvation is in his strength and rests in his refuge. Then and only then will we share his wisdom.

Psalm 91 has always been a favorite of mine. The painting it portrays, of being in the shadow of the Almighty, is what I saw in Granny Adleane, Darlene, Stella, Mary, and Beth. You have to be really close to someone to sit in their shadow. Let's look at what Psalm 91 says:

He that dwelleth in the secret place of the most High shall abide under the shadow of the Almighty. I will say of the LORD, He is my refuge and my fortress: my God; in him will I trust. Surely he shall deliver thee from the snare of the fowler, and from the noisome pestilence.

He shall cover thee with his feathers, and under his wings shalt thou trust: his truth shall be thy shield and buckler. Thou shalt not be afraid for the terror by night; nor for the arrow that flieth by day; Nor for the pestilence that walketh in darkness; nor for the destruction that wasteth at noonday. A thousand shall fall at thy side, and ten thousand at thy right hand; but it shall not come nigh thee. Only with thine eyes shalt thou behold and see the reward of the wicked.

Because thou hast made the LORD, which is my refuge, even the most High, thy habitation; There shall no evil befall thee, neither shall any plague come nigh thy dwelling. For he shall give his angels charge over thee, to keep thee in all thy ways. They shall bear thee up in their hands, lest thou dash thy foot against a stone.

Thou shalt tread upon the lion and adder: the young lion and the dragon shalt thou trample under feet. Because he hath set his love upon me, therefore will I deliver him: I will set him on high, because he hath known my name. He shall call upon me, and I will answer him: I will be with him in trouble; I will deliver him, and honour him.

I am certain you never heard of these women (Granny, Adleane, Darlene, Stella, Mary, and Beth) until now. Yet, these women are true heroines. They help fill the bleachers of faith described in Hebrews. These Elect Women are the individuals whose personal influences qualify them for a seat in heaven's grandstand. They love God. They are outrageously courageous. They have lived lives of endurance and obedience. Eternal perspective has been their way of living. They depend on God for all, and they're unquestionably self-controlled.

"The Lord will guide you always; he will satisfy your needs in a sun-scorched land and will strengthen your frame. You will be like a well-watered garden,

like a spring whose waters never fail. Your people will rebuild the ancient ruins and will raise up the age-old foundations; you will be called repairer of broken walls, restorer of streets with dwellings" (Isaiah 58:11-12 NIV).

Promise Three

TO BROADCAST YOUR VOICE AND YOUR TESTIMONIES, DEAR LORD, SO OTHER WOMEN WILL HEAR YOU MORE CLEARLY, EXPERIENCING HOPE AND INSPIRATION

This chapter brings our attention to the testimonies of myself Kiki Thomas, Granny Adleane, Tony and Kiantki, and Darlene, all of whose testimonies will inspire, challenge, and help broadcast the Word of God.

TESTIMONY ONE: DR. KIKI THOMAS

I live in Atlanta, Georgia. Living in the South, I can tell you about sun-scorched territory. There are times in Atlanta—especially in the summer—when everything looks the same. I wish I could say that every day of your life will be like a day at Stone Mountain Park. Not the kind of place where you get taken away by beautiful walks on the beach in Montego Bay, Jamaica, but the kind of park where you just take it easy. I wish I could say to you that you'll wake up every day ready to have a long, relaxed time with Jesus.

However, at some point along the journey through this book, I feel that most of us will reach sun-scorched territory where we may not feel much spiritual growth. Do you allow Jesus to guide and direct you? Or do you turn back to your old way of handling life's inevitable pain? Anyone can follow God when things are going great, but God offers a promise to those who continue to follow him when life is most difficult. God says in his Word that he will strengthen and make us like a well-watered garden.

In other words, God will give us what we need in order to grow, develop and mature. He helps us grow so we can make a difference in the lives of others. God even allows us to make a difference in our families, our workplaces, our communities and our churches.

One thing is for sure: Jesus is unconventional. He will work in ways we may not understand at all. He is big enough to do things we label *impossible*. He has the power. He has plenty of time. He is so much bigger than any situation. Trust him for more than what you see. Trust him for more than what you feel. He can handle it. He is so confident of his own plans. He can do all things but fail. God is not in the box. He is OUT of any conventional, traditional or expected box.

As you stand on his promises, you'll discover that people will come to you when they are experiencing crises. I have found so much truth here. For example, I have many friends here in Atlanta coming to my door––the front, back and even side door and some on the telephone––asking me to pray for them. "Let's pray about the cancer diagnosis," they say, or the colon cancer diagnosis. I feel blessed that I can help with prayer and the confidence and knowledge of the God who answers our prayer. I love it! I say, "To God be the glory now and forever more!"

I had the opportunity to come together with some of these friends, acquaintances and associates in a Bible study group. It was an amazing experience. God gave me his Word with all of his promises to share with these hurting, God-fearing people. I did what I thought best through Christ and, for me, that was prayer (the Lord's Prayer and my own prayers). I always tried to make my prayers applicable to the problem. I wanted to direct them to God, the One who can guide his children through a sun-scorched land. I believe in an evangelistic method. I also try to keep it subtle.

We live in a fast-paced society, and my Atlanta seems so very fast. It is a society of its own, filled with unexpected situations, concerns, issues and real-people problems. Heartaches and anxieties don't have to be the defining qualities of our daily lives. For Dr. Kiki Thomas, my remedy is this: as we become more connected to God and learn to let go of our vexing emotions, to let go of our grief over life's disasters, pains and ugliness, and as we allow God's peace to enter us, then and only then can we face our experiences with faith. But keep in mind that these qualities don't come from our own efforts. They only come as we trust in the power of the living God. *Praise God!*

Psalm 107:10-15 says:

> *Such as sit in darkness and in the shadow of death, being bound in affliction and iron; Because they rebelled against the words of God, and contemned the counsel of the most High: Therefore he brought down their heart with labour; they fell down, and there was none to help.*

> *Then they cried unto the LORD in their trouble, and he saved them out of their distresses. He brought them*

out of darkness and the shadow of death, and brake
their bands in sunder. Oh that men would praise the
LORD for his goodness, and for his wonderful works
to the children of men!

This psalm lists so many of the prisons from which God has already set us free. This is a psalm of hope; one that gives us encouragement that no matter how deep our pit, God, yes God, can free us.

The key -
whether we are in a maximum security prison,
a prison of our own making,
or a prison that was built around us -
is to thirst for the Almighty Jehovah, God.

He is the only One who holds the key to unlock our chains.

One day following my son's tennis match, my heart cried out to God on his behalf. He had won the match, yet was cheated out of the win. My heart ached for my child as he left the court feeling frustrated and rejected. I said, "God, please protect him, love on him, fix it for him, give him your gift." Later that day, I came across a scripture that spoke of ordained gifts.

"Now there are diversities of gifts, but the same Spirit.
But the manifestation of the Spirit is given to every
man to profit withal. For to one is given by the Spirit
the word of wisdom; to another the word of knowledge
by the same Spirit; To another faith by the same
Spirit; to another the gifts of healing by the same
Spirit" (1 Corinthians 12:4, 7-9).

After reading this scripture, I knew that God had allowed my son and me that measure of faith to enter our souls at that crisis time. I knew I had been granted a huge amount of God's faithfulness and his extreme measure of faith.

These verses talk about special spiritual gifts of faith incorporated by the Spirit of God. This faith enables one to completely trust the truthfulness of God. Only faith through Christ Jesus promotes this kind of trust.

When I read this passage, I stopped immediately in my tracks and said, "Lord Jesus, please give me this added, shared, extreme faith. When the devil sends tests, trials, worries and curve balls, when the roller coaster rides get me really down, I stop and ask God for his Holy Spirit." I say, "I need your Holy Spirit right now, Lord Jesus. I need your shared faith now. The Word says that you give special faith to some. Lord Jesus, I want some, PLEASE! Thank you! I want it all. All, Lord Jesus, you've got to give."

I can't say to you that all my fears disappear with that special prayer, but I can share that I started to receive a greater capacity in my Spirit to believe God for whatever I needed whenever I needed it. As I opened my heart to the Lord, my worries became more manageable.

As you open yourself to the Lord, your troubled areas will become manageable as well. In the process, it became clearer to me that faith and fear are powerful connectors. Faith doesn't necessarily make all our fears go away, but it does empower. Again, I say it empowers us to be people of strength who can and will tolerate tough times and cope with life's difficulties. As Dr. Schuller says, "Tough times never last; tough people do."

Some time later, I attended a women's Bible study group at Fellowship of Faith International Church (Pastor Wayne Thompson) where one courageous, spirit-filled sister, Marlene Matthews, led the study group and used the word fear. Marlene said, "Fear is nothing more than false evidence appearing real." That knocked me to the floor. I was so amazed! I'd never heard it spoken in that manner before. That was so powerful that I had to ask her to repeat it for me. When she did, I was stunned. Once I grasped it, I realized the scope of God's amazing grace, and I became liberated.

She continued to share more about faith. She said that we Elect Women of God need to be more oriented towards God during the good in our lives, not only during the bad. God loves us and wants us always in all ways. He said, "I have loved you with an everlasting love: I have drawn you with loving kindness" (Jeremiah 31:3 NIV), and "For I am persuaded, that neither death, nor life, nor angels, nor principalities, nor powers, nor things present, nor things to come, Nor height, nor depth, nor any other creature, shall be able to separate us from the love of God, which is in Christ Jesus our Lord" (Romans 8:38,39).

I, Dr. Kiki Thomas, have as a vital part of the story of my life the discovery in my heart and soul that God wants us to trust him always. That's real faith. In other words, we are not to be double-minded people. I believe that when I'm troubled and feeling vexed it is time to raise my hands and surrender it all to my Lord and Savior. Then I say, "God, no matter what I'm going through, I am going to trust in you. Thank you for your mercy."

> And when Jesus was entered into Capernaum, there came unto him a centurion, beseeching him, And saying, Lord, my servant lieth at home sick of the palsy, grievously tormented. And Jesus saith unto him, I will come and heal him. The centurion answered and said, Lord, I am not worthy that thou shouldest come under my roof: but speak the word only, and my servant shall be healed.
>
> For I am a man under authority, having soldiers under me: and I say to this man, Go, and he goeth; and to

another, Come, and he cometh; and to my servant,
Do this, and he doeth it. When Jesus heard it, he
marvelled, and said to them that followed, Verily I
say unto you, I have not found so great faith, no, not
in Israel (Matthew 8:5-10).

During Marlene Matthews' Bible study, I immediately read and recorded this particular scripture, and I wondered what Jesus saw in this man's heart. He wasn't all we would think. Or, as the young people say, he wasn't "all of that." I continued to ponder this scripture to find out why the man received so much from Jesus. What did Jesus see in the soldier? After a time, I finally realized that Jesus was impressed with the soldier's response to him. It says the soldier called him Lord.

This man was aware of the laws. He helped the emperor enforce them. He knew that calling Jesus Lord was special. The Bible tells us that the soldier was a highly ranked officer. He was wealthy and had much power. Yet, in using these words about Jesus, he risked losing all his wealth and power.

Yes, this Roman soldier had faith. This story shows us that God doesn't want a place in your life. God wants all of your life. He wants his children to believe in him and his ability to care for us. God wants us to surrender to him only. God wants us to have an attitude of gratitude. When we are experiencing hardships, as we all sometimes do, our attitude and confidence become disturbed. God's promises help us stand. They help us maintain an attitude of faith. When there is much stress and many storms, God's promises are always there.

God, where are you now?
Do ya really love me, God?
Are you really in control, God?

How can good come out of this horrible
thing that has happened to me?

Anxiety tends to cloud our perceptions. Worry takes away from our spirit—physically, emotionally, spiritually. We worry about our health, our marriage, our children. We worry about our job, our retirement and death. The list is endless. At times, I worry myself to the bare core. I'm not certain why, but I do. Please take the time to allow a little grace. Yes, grace. Please give time to figure out those thoughts and feelings and don't forget to give God time to restore you.

My Prayer:
Lord Jesus, show me when my mind and thoughts
are foggy and do not please you.
Create in me a clean heart. Cleanse me and lead me to your peace
as described in Psalm 23:

> *The Lord is my shepherd: I shall not want He maketh*
> *me lie down in green pastures: He leadeth me beside*
> *the still waters. He restoreth my soul: He leadeth me*
> *in the paths of righteousness For his name's sake.*
> *Yea, though I walk through the valley of the shadow*
> *of death, I will fear no evil: For thou art with me: Thy*
> *rod and thy staff, they comfort me. Thou preparest*
> *a table before me in the presence of mine enemies:*
> *Thou anointest my head with oil: my cup runneth*
> *over. Surely goodness and mercy shall follow me all*
> *the days of my life: And I will dwell in the house of*
> *the Lord forever. Amen.*

At 26-years old, my son went on tennis tour. He's an ATP tour tennis pro. I still find myself calling on God to grant my household and especially my son, Kiantki, the gift of faith. I want him to know that this is God's plan for his life.

Every now and then when things get tough, they really do get me down. I go back to God's promises and know that they are all gifts.

Surrendering to God's way and God's purpose is all I will ever need in my life. Life has a way of getting us down at one time or another. We all experience good days and not-so-good days. Sometimes we even go through a season of despair as we endure stressful experiences. Some people become so depressed they can't function at all. We get frustrated with people who betray us or disappoint us, and that leaves us emotionally drained.

When those old worries come and I begin to feel frustrated and negative, I calm myself down and encourage myself by making my faith statement from Psalm 77. Now, don't think that whenever I feel depressed reading Psalm 77 dissolves all my cares. It's not that simple. Some people who are chronic in their despair may need professional Christ-centered counselors. For me, most times all I need is a fresh time with my Daddy, Father God. That's what Psalm 77 gives me. Look at the gifts in this Psalm:

Gift One: Cry Out to God.

> I cried unto God with my voice, even unto God with my voice; and he gave ear unto me. In the day of my trouble I sought the Lord: my sore ran in the night, and ceased not: my soul refused to be comforted. I remembered God, and was troubled: I complained, and my spirit was overwhelmed. Selah (vs. 1-3).

Gift Two: Recall Past Blessings.

> Thou holdest mine eyes waking: I am so troubled that I cannot speak. I have considered the days of old, the years of ancient times. I call to remembrance my song in the night: I commune with mine own heart: and my spirit made diligent search (vs. 4-6).

Gift Three: Ask God the Hard Questions.

Will the Lord cast off for ever? and will he be favourable no more? Is his mercy clean gone for ever? doth his promise fail for evermore? Hath God forgotten to be gracious? hath he in anger shut up his tender mercies? Selah (vs. 7-9).

Gift Four: Choose to Redirect Your Thoughts.

And I said, This is my infirmity: but I will remember the years of the right hand of the most High. I will remember the works of the LORD: surely I will remember thy wonders of old. I will meditate also of all thy work, and talk of thy doings (vs. 10-12).

Gift Five: Magnify God to Diminish Your Problems.

Thy way, O God, is in the sanctuary: who is so great a God as our God?

Thou art the God that doest wonders: thou hast declared thy strength among the people. Thou hast with thine arm redeemed thy people, the sons of Jacob and Joseph. Selah. The waters saw thee, O God, the waters saw thee; they were afraid: the depths also were troubled. The clouds poured out water: the skies sent out a sound: thine arrows also went abroad. The voice of thy thunder was in the heaven: the lightnings lightened the world: the earth trembled and shook (vs. 13-18).

Gift Six: Trust God to Be Your Deliverer.

Thy way is in the sea, and thy path in the great waters, and thy footsteps are not known. Thou leddest thy people like a flock by the hand of Moses and Aaron (vs. 19-20).

**I have discovered in my life that,
while sadness and despair are debilitating,
God is bigger than either of the two when I seek his face
and remember to trust his word and all of his promises.**

**There is a way.
God is the way.**

The battle of faith against fear is conducted in the mind. Fearful thoughts mess with the mind, body, and soul in so many different ways. Faith-filled thoughts bring God's peace to those who listen to the Word and hear the call of God in their hearts. When you are in the midst of trouble, fear says to you, "God is not with you any longer. Where is your Jesus? He doesn't care about little old you. You are left all alone. Funny. HA, HA."

Faith comes along and says, "All God's promises are true." One of my favorite scriptures is Jeremiah 29:11. "For I know the thoughts that I think toward you, saith the Lord, thoughts of peace, and not of evil, to give you an expected end." I am reminded that he does, indeed, have plans for me, for you, and for all of us. Personally and professionally, we are on God's drawing board. He has a plan and a purpose for your life. God said he would never leave you alone. Trust him when someone has truly disappointed you.

Fear says, "You can't trust them."
Faith says, "My God is real. He's more than a conqueror."

When you have been waiting for something over a period of time - we all experience that -

Fear says, "You're going to be too old when it comes."

Faith says, "I'm trusting in God. He's never late. Thank you, Jesus."

When you are experiencing trial after trial, test after test. When you're on a roller coaster ride with many problems,

> Fear says, "If God cared about you, he would not put you through all of this."
> Faith says, "All things work together for good for those who love the Lord and are called according to his purpose."

I share all of this
from my life and heart and soul
to join with you in inspiration and faith.

Remember that our worries, our issues, stress, and our situations don't amaze God. Trusting Jesus is a good habit. The benefits are numerous. So, let us now hold fast to the Word of God. We are the children of the Most High. We have joy that can never fail and so much more. "The fear of the Lord is the beginning of knowledge: but fools despise wisdom and instruction" (Proverbs 1:7). The fear of the Lord prolongs life. The fear of the Lord leads to life so that one may sleep.

In Proverbs 14:26 we read, "In the fear of the Lord is strong confidence: and his children shall have a place of refuge." What an awesome promise that can fuel our trust in him. One thing for certain, we have a promise for our future. This we learn through Job 23:10, "But he knoweth the way that I take: when he hath tried me, I shall come forth as gold."

We must not forget to remember. We must remind ourselves of what the Lord has already done, and what he will continue to do according to his promises. Trusting him doesn't mean our trials will vanish. It does mean we will always have a Father to talk with. Trusting him is all we need in life. Praise him in all of his glory. I will praise the Lord with everything that is in me. *Praise him!*

Walking with the Lord does not offer a simple solution to our issues and problems. It is not just, "Don't sweat the small stuff." God is in the small stuff, big stuff, all of our stuff. God is in control always. He will care for me and for you. The peace that God gives to his disciples is not the absence of trials but rather the confidence that when we walk through hardship, he will walk right along with us. In time of need, we can turn to him. He wants us to talk to him. He doesn't need lots of words. He doesn't need a book about our life. He only wants our attention. He wants our heart.

If you feel far away from him, move in a little closer. The Bible says, "Draw near to God and he will draw near to you" (James 4:8).

I have found this in my own life, and I wanted to share it. I have learned that God's presence has such an awesome, calming effect. God is always in control. So, remain in his Word over time. The longer I walk with him and talk with him, the more confidence I have that he is truly trustworthy. He is the One I can trust to hold the rope to get me back onto the boat. Thank you, Jesus. We all can have joy in spite of our challenges.

> *My brethren, count it all joy when ye fall into divers temptations; Knowing this, that the trying of your faith worketh patience. But let patience have her perfect work, that ye may be perfect and entire, wanting nothing. If any of you lack wisdom, let him ask of God, that giveth to all men liberally, and upbraideth not; and it shall be given him* (James 1:2-5).

> *Wherein ye greatly rejoice, though now for a season, if need be, ye are in heaviness through manifold temptations: That the trial of your faith, being much*

more precious than of gold that perisheth, though it be tried with fire, might be found unto praise and honour and glory at the appearing of Jesus Christ: Whom having not seen, ye love; in whom, though now ye see him not, yet believing, ye rejoice with joy unspeakable and full of glory: Receiving the end of your faith, even the salvation of your souls (1 Peter 1:6-9).

And blessed is she that believed: for there shall be a performance of those things which were told her from the Lord. And Mary said, My soul doth magnify the Lord, And my spirit hath rejoiced in God my Saviour (Luke 1:45-47).

He staggered not at the promise of God through unbelief; but was strong in faith, giving glory to God; And being fully persuaded that, what he had promised, he was able also to perform (Romans 4:20, 21).

As I end the story about my life and lessons that I have learned, please pray with me:

Father God, in the name of Jesus we come here to praise you and to honor you. Father God, we thank you for this time. This day we pray, Father God, that we are in need of more faith, more so that we can meet this challenge and so we can find ways to develop more faith through Christ Jesus. Thank you, Lord, for giving us the truth so we can trust in you, believe in you and know, Father God, that you are always there. No matter what hardships, you are there. We know that where you are, we are, and that you will surround us, protect us, enfold us, and always be watching over us. You know about all different situations and have the plan to help us through and learn and profit from them. We love you, Father God, and we know you will bring us peace in the name of Jesus. Amen.

Most of what I am about to write deals with faithful, God-fearing women and men, mentors of mine.

> Then Naomi her mother in law said unto her, My daughter, shall I not seek rest for thee, that it may be well with thee? And now is not Boaz of our kindred, with whose maidens thou wast? Behold, he winnoweth barley to night in the threshingfloor. Wash thyself therefore, and anoint thee, and put thy raiment upon thee, and get thee down to the floor: but make not thyself known unto the man, until he shall have done eating and drinking. And it shall be, when he lieth down, that thou shalt mark the place where he shall lie, and thou shalt go in, and uncover his feet, and lay thee down; and he will tell thee what thou shalt do. And she said unto her, All that thou sayest unto me I will do (Ruth 3:1-5).

I am so blessed to have several women in my life and in my church and in my circles who are role models for me and for others. They show God's calling with Christ-like behavior and godly ways. I want to take time here to describe these Elect Women of God so that we all can benefit from their modeling. I begin by sharing my family and home, what they do, how they do and act––what makes them.

My granny, Adleane Wilson (grandmother on my mother's [Mary's] side of the family tree.) Granny, Mommy––we called her both of those. For this publication, I will say Granny Adleane. Granny was so special to me; she was someone I will always love, remember and appreciate. I want to be able to keep her memories alive for generations to come with testimonies of her love for her family and friends, her delicious Louisiana cooking and more.

TESTIMONY TWO: GRANNY ADLEANE

Here I will share a glimpse of our family. Granny Adleane always communicated love to all of us. My wonderful Aunt Darlene was Granny's sister. She was the strong one for all of us. Aunt Stella, better known as Bo, was always rich, giving, and loving. It was a real blessing to sit and listen to her words of wisdom and the lessons she taught. As a child, I spent much time with Bo. She was my Grandmother Adleane's mother. (Granny Adleane's birth mother died when Granny was a baby, and Bo became her mother). My mom's (Mary's) unfailing love was always there, even as I write this book. And Nanna Beth, better known as Betty, has always had so much hope and belief in me. I love all these Elect ladies. The tree was and still is strong. It is still rooted and grounded on the Word of God.

Granny Adleane was truly a powerful prayer warrior, a woman with a lot of God's grace and his mercy. She shared a lot of God's Word with her own children—Mary, Betty, and Jesse—also with all her grandchildren. She was a true Proverbs 31 woman. She spent much time in prayer and with her family. She worked diligently from sunup to sundown. We were so privileged to have her with us. She shared so much love and taught us so much about loving God.

The family was blessed to own their own businesses. They owned and operated a restaurant. The restaurant and bar is now our family-owned Christian bookstore and supply store. You can check out more about the store at FandAChristianBookstore.com.

My grandmother spent most of her time operating that business from day to day. She also cared for her grandchildren and other children in the neighborhood. She was a woman who enjoyed preparing food for everyone. The restaurant allowed her and other family members to do lots of cooking and sharing. There will be a taste of Louisiana by Granny and company at the end of the book, including some of those delicious, Louisiana recipe favorites.

Granny believed that cooking was a way to show love. To sit at the dinner table and share stories and look at old photographs was such a delight. I learned volumes from Granny, as did the other family members and even neighborhood children. Dinnertime was a significant event. There could never be too much food and drink, and there was always more than enough for all.

Granny Adleane's generosity was amazing. She spent many long hours in that restaurant cooking for her family, friends, and other families in the community. She was awesome with both her preparation and presentation of food. She made food an inspiring and loving event—a day to remember. Favorite recipes that captured my soul were her kindness mixed with green beans and mashed potatoes, Louisiana-style rice dressing with lots of chicken giblets and livers, and baked chicken with lots of lemon juice. Her love was the spice for each dish.

She topped off meals with her special dessert: strawberry shortcake. I don't mean cake from a grocery store. I am referring to the real deal—home-baked bread and freshly picked, cut, and cleaned strawberries. (Nothing was microwaved; all from the original.) These delicious meals were served daily, not just at special times.

The weeks around Good Friday and Easter Sunday were, wow....a real blessing! Don't let me forget to share all about her delicious, fantastic crawfish bisque (sure nuff Louisiana)...always served with the blessing said before every meal.

Yet, even with all of that preparation and cooking, she still made time to share God's words with others and especially with me. She worked with all her body and soul. At the same time, she was giving praise to God Almighty.

They sold all kinds of stuff in the store, from food to general and household items. Oh, what a woman of God Adleane was! All of those family women were driven to do good no matter what the issues were. A sweet good group of dedicated women, they believed in only God's best for themselves, their families, and others.

Adleane was married to Frank Wilson. God blessed them with two daughters and one son (Mary, Betty, and their son, Jesse). Praise God, Mary and Jesse are still in good health in Louisiana. Nanna Beth––unfortunately suffering from Alzheimer's––is in a nursing home in Plaquemine, Louisiana. Mary owns and operates the Christian bookstore daily. You can check her on the web at FandAchristianstore.com.

Mary married Henry Peterson and was blessed with two boys. Henry died early in the marriage. She remarried William Hammond, and that union was blessed with me. This marriage ended in divorce. Then, Mary married Warren Rylander and was blessed with two girls: Cookie and Wanda. Warren died of lung cancer. My mother married once again to Lloyd Young. Praise God, they are still living happily together in Plaquemine, Louisiana.

Adleane's second daughter, Betty, married Isaiah Edwards. They had three daughters and three sons: Diane, Jean, Jeanette, Thomas, Isaiah, and Bruce.

Adleane's son, Jesse, married Ethel Lego. They were blessed with four boys and three daughters: Jesse Jr., Gerald, Jackie, Frank, Pamela, Sandra (deceased 1996), and Marilyn. This is just a brief view of Frank and Adleane's seed.

I have always seen Granny Adleane as my strong, capable, self-sufficient and invincible Granny. She had resilience and was able to respond to what life brought her without it "doing her in." Granny never took credit for being strong, though. She often would say, "I think God has shown himself to me in a special kind of way."

I am sure as a reader you wish he would be so kind and do that for you. If she were here, she would say something like this, "I'm not sure I can put it into words. It is that deep inside feeling that gives you joy, and you know that you didn't put it there."

We think that *strong* means to be hard and unable to be hurt. That is not it. Strength is more about being able to bear hurt. That comes from knowing whose hands we're in. "I lift up my eyes to the hills," wrote the psalmist. "Where does my help come from? My help comes from the Lord, the maker of heaven and earth" (Psalm 121:1,2). This psalm is from the Songs of Ascent, hymns that were sung by the Jewish people each year to encourage themselves on the long journey to Jerusalem during Passover week. Scattered among the hills surrounding the city were many heathen temples. The words of this psalm served to remind the worshipers of the one true God who is the true source of power.

Where does your help come from?
One distinctive quality in the lives of believers
is readiness to admit they can't help themselves.

"In fact, I will boast in my weakness," wrote Paul. "For when I am weak, then God is strong" (2 Corinthians 12:10 paraphrased).

Granny loved her children. She loved her family. She loved the Lord. She was a teacher from the heart. She would teach and train other women—especially new mothers—about the Word of God, about tasks, responsibilities, and the privileges of motherhood. She was the one to teach the young women about loving their children unconditionally in every way—practically, physically, socially, morally, and spiritually.

Even back then, she taught young mothers about parenting. With all her work and sharing with others and her family, I think about women in the Bible like Sarah, Rebecca, Hannah, Samson's mother, and Elizabeth, just to name a few. These women knew that children were a blessing from God.

Granny was a woman who served God with her whole life by shaping the lives of others for Christ. She would say very devoutly that there are steps to loving your loved ones, children and all:

- Always be ready to teach them, since it is not the school's responsibility. This role belongs primarily to the parents.
- Train them. They must be taught to respect and to cooperate with others.
- Talk to God about them, and talk to them about the Lord.
- Take time to read to them. Read them God's Word and classical literature.
- Teach prayer. Start with the prayer of Jesus.
- Take good care of them.
- Tell them about Jesus.

She talked about God's power. Often, she would say, "God does not give me power. He exercises his power through me." What is power? Power is the ability to produce a desired effect. She felt that prayer was the source of power. The best gift is a good example and, for her, the best example she gave us was her life of prayer. Granny faithfully and lovingly taught and trained her children. She taught others how to pray to the Lord Jesus.

As a wife, she helped her husband with his responsibilities, his tasks, his roles, and his work. She followed her husband in each and every way as his helpmate. She submitted to him. Titus 2:5 says, "To be discreet, chaste, keepers at home, good, obedient to their own husbands, that the word of God be not blasphemed." This tells us how important it is to be submissive and follow our husband. Paul wrote volumes about this.

Granny showed high regard for her husband. She loved him with all her heart. She took good care of him. I will never forget how she would put him ahead of herself. Ouch! As a young teenager full of my own selfishness, that was often hard for me to understand. Praise God. Thank him for wisdom. Now I really understand. Thanks be to God.

This woman of God meant so much to me; she meant so much to all of us. She was truly a woman after God's heart. She offered much time to the family, to their business, but most of all she and her family spent much time in God's house. She taught us to grow up, and in growing up to love the Lord and to serve him so that we may continue the legacy for generations to come. She was very involved, active and a part of her local church, Ebenezer Baptist Church. She was dedicated to her church and to her community at large. She was a big servant for the Lord God.

Granny would allow me to help her bake and cook. I always enjoyed working with her in her big kitchen. Her kitchen was the school of culinary arts for all her children and grands. Fortunately, in our family, cooking was viewed as necessary. (Remember we owned the restaurant.) Granny was the queen of her home, queen of the restaurant, and, most of all, she was one of God's special ladies.

In so many ways, she made home and caring for her home a number one priority. Titus 2:3-5 says:

> *The aged women likewise, that they be in behaviour as becometh holiness, not false accusers, not given to much wine, teachers of good things; That they may teach the young women to be sober, to love their husbands, to love their children, To be discreet,*

chaste, keepers at home, good, obedient to their own
husbands, that the word of God be not blasphemed.

She loved her home and family.
She had a heart for God.

Granny Adleane and Daddy Frank were good
examples of how to trust the Lord.

Proverbs 24:3 NIV says, "Through works her house is built." In James we read, "The wisdom that came from above is first of all pure and full of gentleness. Then comes peace" (James 3:17 TLB). She was always ready to share with me about anything and everything. She shared with me about her role as a wife, a mother, and a grandmother. More importantly, she taught me to be a child of the Kingdom.

She referred many times to the Amplified Version of Proverbs 31, the well-known chapter about the virtuous woman. She loved Proverbs 31 and would often refer to it as her spiritual food for her household. She fed herself daily which strengthened her spiritually, physically, and mentally for her God-given tasks. In her gentle and loving way, she would say, "We don't have to do it all alone because God has PROMISED strength for the day." She would quote Isaiah 41:10 NASV often, "I will strengthen you and keep you. I will uphold you with my righteous mighty hand." God gave her and her daughters the strength as mothers to do what is right and stand with God.

Prayer of Mama Adleane
"Lord, I pray you continue to give me faith and strength
to do what is pleasing to you. I know you
will do what your Word says.
Thank you, Lord, for loving me in Jesus' name."

Granny Adleane would always talk about her safe place. A safe place is to talk to God, tell him about your hurt, anger, disappointments, and even how sad you might feel. She would say, "He already knows the secrets of our hearts." Her prayers never consisted of fancy, religious words. She would share her thoughts and feelings with God as you and I would with a trusted friend.

> *"Prayer is more than words. It's listening, seeing, feeling."*
> Norman Vincent Peale

According to Granny, she saw powerful breakthroughs when she invited the healing presence of God into her heart. In the Psalms, we see that David mastered the art of throwing his pain on the Lord in prayer. He never censored his feelings. He never tried to weigh his words or tried to pretend things were all good when they were not good. David was honest about how he felt, and he poured out his heart to God:

> *Give ear to my prayer, O God; and hide not thyself from my supplication. Attend unto me, and hear me: I mourn in my complaint, and make a noise;*
>
> *My heart is sore pained within me: and the terrors of death are fallen upon me. Fearfulness and trembling are come upon me, and horror hath overwhelmed me. And I said, Oh that I had wings like a dove! for then would I fly away, and be at rest.*
>
> *Let death seize upon them, and let them go down quick into hell: for wickedness is in their dwellings, and among them. As for me, I will call upon God; and the LORD shall save me. Evening, and morning, and at noon, will I pray, and cry aloud: and he shall hear my voice. He hath delivered my soul in peace from the battle that was against me: for there were many with me.*

Cast thy burden upon the LORD, and he shall sustain thee: he shall never suffer the righteous to be moved. Psalm 55:1-2, 4-6, 15-18, 22.

Prayer helps us release our feelings more constructively.

Granny Adleane and her sister, Darlene, shared much joy and pain. They also shared about how to be content in spite of the pain. Granny referred to Paul lots of times because Paul understood that concept He wrote to the church at Philippi informing them that he had learned to be content, whatever the circumstances: "Not that I speak in respect of want: for I have learned, in whatsoever state I am, therewith to be content" (Philippians 4:11). This means that there is still hope for us who have faced discontent.

> *"But godliness with contentment is great gain"* (1Timothy 6:6).

> *"According as his divine power hath given unto us all things that pertain unto life and godliness, through the knowledge of him that hath called us to glory and virtue"* (2 Peter 1:3).

These verses tell us that we have everything we need for life. If this is so, why are so many of us discontent? We come by it naturally. Consider Eve in Genesis 3:6, "And when the woman saw that the tree was good for food, and that it was pleasant to the eyes, and a tree to be desired to make one wise, she took of the fruit thereof, and did eat, and gave also unto her husband with her; and he did eat."

Some women feel certain they would be more contented if they had the house, the bank account, the husband, the children, and a three-car garage. For women of faith, to be content with little is a hard call, but to be content with much is impossible. The more we have, the more we want. This means that if you are richer, you are poorer. We must submit our greed to the Lord Jesus Christ in order to find the joy of contentment. Contentment is found only in the knowledge of God.

There were times of severe pain when Granny Adleane cried out to her Lord and Savior. She felt weak, tired, wounded, and right-out depressed. During those times, she sought him more. She always found time to spend with the Lord to renew her mind and soul. Granny would say, "Study God's Word and be content when you study." She would encourage us to always study his Word. I didn't understand all of that as a young girl. But now: oh, yes! I do.

Studying God's Word has never been as easy as it is today. F and A Christian Bookstore and others have endless guides and aids to help in personal Bible study. Granny would say, "You only need to set aside time to read the Bible with a pencil and pad in hand." As I mature, I have found that when I study God's Word, I come to know and love it. We eat God's words and find them satisfying (Jeremiah 15:16). Spend time with your Bible, pen, and pad.

Granny would often share her upper-room experiences and God's Word with me. She was truly a woman of great contentment; truly a woman after God's heart.

She was a fervent prayer warrior and had many of her prayers answered. I am a living testimony to that. Ouch! Granny prayed for me. There was a time she told me about the prayers she had written and saved for her grands to give to their children. She gave me those prayers, and I still have some of them in my Bible, including those which she gave to me about 45 years ago. They are tattered and worn but still useful and significant to me and my family. This was truly my blessing from her.

She would get her Bible, write out a verse and keep it visual all day long as she did her work at the restaurant. She was as content as

Paul was. Paul wrote from prison that he had learned to be content, whatever the circumstances. He then added, "I can do everything through him who gives me strength" (Philippians 4:13 NASV). Paul applied his knowledge of God to his circumstance, and he was content.

The nugget of spiritual contentment will be yours when all that God is and all that he has done in Christ Jesus fills your heart. We may lack some things in this old world, but as women of faith and women of strength, we must work to develop the nugget of true contentment. This is the will of God for all of us.

Her Faith

> *Therefore I say unto you, What things soever ye desire, when ye pray, believe that ye receive them, and ye shall have them* (Mark 11:24).

> *Fret not thyself because of evildoers, neither be thou envious against the workers of iniquity. For they shall soon be cut down like the grass, and wither as the green herb.*

> *Trust in the LORD, and do good; so shalt thou dwell in the land, and verily thou shalt be fed. Delight thyself also in the LORD; and he shall give thee the desires of thine heart. Commit thy way unto the LORD; trust also in him; and he shall bring it to pass. And he shall bring forth thy righteousness as the light, and thy judgment as the noonday.*

> *Rest in the LORD, and wait patiently for him: fret not thyself because of him who prospereth in his way, because of the man who bringeth wicked devices to pass. Cease from anger, and forsake wrath: fret not*

thyself in any wise to do evil. For evildoers shall be cut off: but those that wait upon the LORD, they shall inherit the earth.

For yet a little while, and the wicked shall not be: yea, thou shalt diligently consider his place, and it shall not be. But the meek shall inherit the earth; and shall delight themselves in the abundance of peace. The wicked plotteth against the just, and gnasheth upon him with his teeth. The Lord shall laugh at him: for he seeth that his day is coming. The wicked have drawn out the sword, and have bent their bow, to cast down the poor and needy, and to slay such as be of upright conversation. Their sword shall enter into their own heart, and their bows shall be broken.

A little that a righteous man hath is better than the riches of many wicked. For the arms of the wicked shall be broken: but the LORD upholdeth the righteous. The LORD knoweth the days of the upright: and their inheritance shall be for ever. They shall not be ashamed in the evil time: and in the days of famine they shall be satisfied. But the wicked shall perish, and the enemies of the LORD shall be as the fat of lambs: they shall consume; into smoke shall they consume away.

The wicked borroweth, and payeth not again: but the righteous sheweth mercy, and giveth. For such as be blessed of him shall inherit the earth; and they that be cursed of him shall be cut off. The steps of a good man are ordered by the LORD: and he delighteth in his way. Though he fall, he shall not be utterly cast down: for the LORD upholdeth him with his hand.

I have been young, and now am old; yet have I not seen the righteous forsaken, nor his seed begging bread. He is ever merciful, and lendeth; and his seed is blessed. Depart from evil, and do good; and dwell for evermore. For the LORD loveth judgment, and forsaketh not his saints; they are preserved for ever: but the seed of the wicked shall be cut off.

The righteous shall inherit the land, and dwell therein for ever. The mouth of the righteous speaketh wisdom, and his tongue talketh of judgment. The law of his God is in his heart; none of his steps shall slide. The wicked watcheth the righteous, and seeketh to slay him. The LORD will not leave him in his hand, nor condemn him when he is judged.

Wait on the LORD, and keep his way, and he shall exalt thee to inherit the land: when the wicked are cut off, thou shalt see it. I have seen the wicked in great power, and spreading himself like a green bay tree. Yet he passed away, and, lo, he was not: yea, I sought him, but he could not be found.

Mark the perfect man, and behold the upright: for the end of that man is peace. But the transgressors shall be destroyed together: the end of the wicked shall be cut off. But the salvation of the righteous is of the LORD: he is their strength in the time of trouble. And the LORD shall help them, and deliver them: he shall deliver them from the wicked, and save them, because they trust in him (Psalm 37).

Granny always said, "Trust and do good work." Hearty trust of him. Her faith was so strong and powerful. She was like an angel. She showed grace and loved all people: red and yellow, black and white.

Like Jesus, all special in her sight. She taught so that we understood each and every word.

She was a most devoted prayer maker. When she thought of people needing prayers, she would add their names to her prayer list. She added pages and pages. She spent many hours in quiet time praying for others. If people would ask her to pray for them, she would jot their name on her little tattered sheet. She would pray, and she always wanted to know the results for those she prayed for. As stated earlier, she prayed very hard for her family. Her prayers were short and from the heart.

I like to connect Granny's faith with the book of Esther. Granny Adleane made a statement that made a great impact on me, "I can tell Jesus anything and know for sure he would not allow anyone or anything to come between him and me." She frequently sang the old hymn, "What a Friend We Have in Jesus." I didn't understand its value until my adult years.

Thank you, Granny, for always being there for me. I thank God for his grace and his mercies each and every day. Even when I feel he is taking such a long time, I know that our time is not his time. He can do whatever, whenever, to whomever he chooses.

Confessing my own impatience is tough. I'm finally learning to release my trials and confess all the stuff that has held me hostage for so long. Now I feel free as a bird. Oh, thank you, Lord Jesus. I learned from Granny to worship him with praise and thanksgiving always, singing songs of praise early in the morning and even during noonday and at night, exalting him because there is no other. He is the great I AM.

I'm enjoying my new relationship with him, enjoying how he protects me and gives me strength to keep on even when I feel so tired. I say, "Lord, give me strength," and he does just that. As the Word says in Nehemiah 8:10, "The joy of the Lord is my strength."

When discussing God-given strength, I often think of the family women who have gone on to be with the Lord. I come back again and again to my Granny, Aunt Darlene, Great-aunt Stella, my mom, and Nanna Beth. There are also others too numerous to list. The women who are still with us include my precious and loving mother, Rose Mary, my Aunt Betty (who is now suffering from Alzheimer's disease), my two biological sisters, Cookie and Wanda, all of who are women of strength in spite of the odds. There are also my sisters-in-law, Carolyn and Elizabeth, my mother-in-law, Emma Lee, my sister-in-law, Yvette, cohorts of mine, and so many female acquaintances. God bless them all in the name of Jesus. I often ask my Savior to give me a double portion of strength when I pray for these jewels.

TESTIMONY THREE: TONY AND KIANTKI

"Your rod and your staff shall comfort me" (Psalm 23:4).

Early on a summer day my son and I were at a hotel in Florida on a tennis trip. I was awakened real early and started to pray. I was led to the 23rd Psalm because so much was going on in my life that I wasn't sure where to turn or where to go so. I didn't know then what I know now. I was totally exhausted, and I had not even started my day. I had really looked forward to this trip because it was now summer, and I was free from my responsibilities as a professor. I had the entire summer to run the tennis juniors' circuit with my one and only child, Kiantki. I started to cry. I thought I was quiet with my crying, but I was not.

Kiantki woke up and said to me, "Mom, are you okay?" Being me, I smiled and said yes, that everything was good. You know, God used my one and only son, Kiantki. Kiantki was God's strength to me at that moment. I leaned on him until I was able to regain control. After a while, he got up and got ready for his tennis match. I got ready as well and joined him for breakfast before he went to play the match.

He played a tremendous game. I was happy for him and felt so much better deep within, in spite of my own stressors and pain. I completed that trip with an unusual sense of fulfillment and many blessings. Not only did I sense God's presence in my life in a special way, but I was so grateful to God for using my child to give me a word of support in a moment when life appeared to me to be a bit just too much.

I was reminded that I don't always have to be strong. In fact, God doesn't want me to be strong as those out there in the world define strength. He wants me, and he wants you to lean on him always. He wants me, and he wants you to lean on him as the shepherd leans on his staff. He wants me, and he wants you to be comforted by his power, not to depend on self, but to depend on him. The Lord's strength is made perfect in weakness.

It is so true, but we tend to forget that God does want us to be weak so that he can be strong. God wants us to know that we are weak and without him we'll become weaker. God is good. He is not in need of our help.

This reminds me of the new piece that is out today where God says that he is taking over all today and doesn't need your help; so, relax and get a cup of herbal tea. He says, "I am in charge, and I don't need any help." The real point here is not weakness or strength, but to get a clear picture that God is God. We are all driven by much fear of this and fear of that, whatever this or that may be—bills, marriage and family problems, aging parents, children, violence, suicide, homicide, all the stuff that comes to destroy our joy. But we must hold on to God's hand and remember that in spite of what we see, "The joy of the Lord is my strength" (Nehemiah 8:10 NIV).

We want to believe that we are strong. We fear that others will talk about us in ways that are not becoming. We need our shell. We need our confidence. Yet, when we try to be strong on our own, we end up failing again and again. We show just how weak we really are. We get out of control, bitter, and stiff-necked. We must take God's path and allow him to be God, allow him to take all our garbage and be the strong; one to whom we admit our weaknesses. He can give us strength that surpasses all others.

God gives us strength each and every day.

There are lessons to be learned from each experience in our lives.

God gives us strength to keep moving on during times when we think we cannot. Usually those lessons are God telling us that it is time to slow down. During this past semester, I had a severe pain in my left shoulder. I had experienced this pain about a year ago, but was alright with a physician visit and physical therapy. When the pain returned this past semester, I said, "Lord, what is this that are you telling me here?" I stopped all those extracurricular activities and started to take time for me and prayed for my healing. And those darling women of strength whom I mentioned earlier also prayed for my healing. My arm was miraculously healed. Often the strength comes from other people.

So many times, their love and strength put me back in touch with my own strength. I particularly value my husband and my son. I have begun to realize we all take turns being strong for each other. I've seen this with special clarity in the past two years, as we struggled to cope with the high cost of our son's tennis tour. We have been weak and, at the same time, strong.

When my husband is really upset and feels he can't tolerate what's going on, I seem to handle the setting better by praying more or keeping my connection with those in prayer, usually my mother and my sisters, Cookie and Wanda.

Then when I have had it and can't take any more, Tony and Kiantki will be holding on and holding steady. This is very natural for us. There are times when my son is as far away as Europe and calls to ask if everything is alright. The Spirit has, at times, caused my son to call. Then we pray, and I always encourage him to hold on to Psalm 9:11 in The Living Bible. He laughs at me because he says that my telling him is his strength. We live within the shadow of the Almighty sheltered by the God who is above all gods. I have my son say the psalms each day so that he can have God's Word right with him and so can I.

> *This I declare, that he alone is my refuge, my place of safety. He is my God and I am trusting him* (Psalm 91:1 TLB).

> *We take turns being God's strength to each other as we care for those we love.*

God's strength is available to all of us all the time, not just when crises arise. When we spend time with him and lean on him in daily prayer, then we will grow stronger. I am able to handle whatever comes my way. I am better equipped for what tomorrow brings. God wants us strong, but––better yet––he wants us to obey. I have to say yes to Jesus and obey his leading and teaching if I want this walk of strength. He gave the order so that I know he will provide me with the strength to carry out those orders.

The songs that were shared with me when I was younger appear to have more truth to me as an adult. I remember that song saying, "We are weak but thou art strong." He is ready to fill us with his strength. He will take all our weaknesses and turn them into strengths. This is seen in these passages:

> *Blessed is the man whose strength is in thee; in whose heart are the ways of them* (Psalms 84:5).

> *The LORD is my light and my salvation; whom shall I fear? the LORD is the strength of my life; of whom shall I be afraid?*

When the wicked, even mine enemies and my foes, came upon me to eat up my flesh, they stumbled and fell. Though an host should encamp against me, my heart shall not fear: though war should rise against me, in this will I be confident.

One thing have I desired of the LORD, that will I seek after; that I may dwell in the house of the LORD all the days of my life, to behold the beauty of the LORD, and to enquire in his temple. For in the time of trouble he shall hide me in his pavilion: in the secret of his tabernacle shall he hide me; he shall set me up upon a rock. And now shall mine head be lifted up above mine enemies round about me: therefore will I offer in his tabernacle sacrifices of joy; I will sing, yea, I will sing praises unto the LORD.

Hear, O LORD, when I cry with my voice: have mercy also upon me, and answer me. When thou saidst, Seek ye my face; my heart said unto thee, Thy face, LORD, will I seek. Hide not thy face far from me; put not thy servant away in anger: thou hast been my help; leave me not, neither forsake me, O God of my salvation.

When my father and my mother forsake me, then the LORD will take me up. Teach me thy way, O LORD, and lead me in a plain path, because of mine enemies. Deliver me not over unto the will of mine enemies: for false witnesses are risen up against me, and such as breathe out cruelty.

I had fainted, unless I had believed to see the goodness of the LORD in the land of the living. Wait on the LORD: be of good courage, and he shall strengthen thine heart: wait, I say, on the LORD (Psalm 27: 1-14).

And he said unto me, My grace is sufficient for thee: for my strength is made perfect in weakness. Most gladly therefore will I rather glory in my infirmities, that the power of Christ may rest upon me (2 Corinthians 12:9).

But I have prayed for thee, that thy faith fail not: and when thou art converted, strengthen thy brethren (Luke 22:32).

Because the foolishness of God is wiser than men; and the weakness of God is stronger than men. For ye see your calling, brethren, how that not many wise men after the flesh, not many mighty, not many noble, are called: But God hath chosen the foolish things of the world to confound the wise; and God hath chosen the weak things of the world to confound the things which are mighty; And base things of the world, and things which are despised, hath God chosen, yea, and things which are not, to bring to nought things that are: That no flesh should glory in his presence (1 Corinthians 1:25-29).

He giveth power to the faint; and to them that have no might he increaseth strength. Even the youths shall faint and be weary, and the young men shall utterly fall: But they that wait upon the LORD shall renew their strength; they shall mount up with wings as eagles; they shall run, and not be weary; and they shall walk, and not faint (Isaiah 40:29-31).

God wants us to wait on him. The Word says, "Wait on the Lord and be of good courage and he shall strengthen thine heart" (Psalm 27:14). Just this past March, I was on my way to our Christian store in Plaquemine, Louisiana to do the annual Vacation Bible School

(VBS) training. This is training we have done for the past four years. During this time, it has grown in big leaps. Again, women of strength found more and better ways to stay in touch with God's Word, and sharing it with the young people at the VBS session.

I had just completed the major travel arrangements and itinerary for my touring tennis-pro son. I regrouped and packed a few clothes and all of the training material, and headed off to Atlanta International Airport for Baton Rouge, Louisiana on a Friday. My sister here had changed plans and was unable to join me, so I went alone anyway.

In the middle of all this activity, I stopped and said, "Now Lord, you're going to have to really give me some fast strength right now." I was exhausted. I got on my knees to pray, and I prayed the prayer of Jesus over and over. I got up and said, "Dear Lord, I've got to go now. My plane leaves in one hour." Thank God that I live around the corner from Atlanta International Airport.

I got a taxi, went to the airport, boarded my plane to Louisiana, and went fast to sleep. I didn't awaken until I landed. My mother and my sister, Cookie, met me at airport with a huge lemonade and a Louisiana Po' Boy sandwich. (I wrote earlier that we love supporting each other, even through food nourishment.) I thanked them for their love, and we went home.

I told them how glad I was to get home. My mother is my strength. She had "praise the Lord music" going, and we celebrated each other as we went on our journey. We arrived home, then immediately went to the building to set up for the VBS training.

Weak but never fainting, I prepared for the training. which had the theme, "In the Race With Jesus." I stopped and started to laugh. I had been reading off and on all month the materials for the training, and I thought you couldn't win this race if you faint. I went to Hebrews 11:1 and started to repeat that verse over and over. My strength was renewed almost immediately! I use this as an example because we are what we say we are. If we are weak and speak aloud that we are strong, then we begin to feel God's power.

Does God want us to be weak so he can be strong? No, that is not it. Simply, we are weak, and he is strong. There is no place in the Word that tells us to be weak and or to be strong. It says for us to look at who we are and who God is and then do the best thing, which is to lean on him and depend on his strength. We know that is much easier said than done, because we are too driven by the world and what it says. Sometimes this strength does come through other people, such as my husband and son giving me strength. Also, my strength came from that group of women attending that VBS training.

The process of becoming strong in the Word and in Jesus takes a lot of energy. Growing strong in him is not just sitting around and waiting until I'm strong so that I can do what he wants me to do. No, it's about doing what I believe God wants me to do––to trust him to give me the strength I need when I need it. God expected me to be obedient, and I have said yes to his leading. Yes, I want to be a strong woman of God.

> *I have to take that leap of faith*
> *and step up to the plate,*
> *trusting in God alone.*

This takes courage. It takes courage to admit to our weaknesses. I often have that feeling when I am in the classroom on the college campus. I have a class of 40 students, and I have that feeling of awe and responsibility to the students in my class. There are times I am weak. I mean so very weak that I feel I don't have the energy to connect with the real source, my Father, but I am usually 100% sure that I am where he wants me to be; so I go on and give that lecture anyway.

When I thank him for the strength, God gives me the strength. He gives me the power I need to get the job done in a way that is pleasing in his sight. There are times when I have much energy, and I sometimes try to go it alone. It is so different when I stop my way and take his way by relying on his strength. I feel better when I decide to lean on him.

And when that happens again and again, I am amazed at how everything falls into his perfect and divine order. Then I find myself drenched in tears. I take no credit for what I do. I give him all the praise and all the glory. Without him, I am nothing. Sometimes God's strength and God's power comes from those I love, like my son and husband, as well as the sister trainers in my training sessions.

The same power and strength is available to you, no matter what you are dealing with or where you are at this juncture in your life. The promise of God's strength applies to each and every one of us, especially for us as women. I often think of a dear friend of mine who suffered such mental stress she was in and out of professional facilities. I can't imagine having to cope with that kind of pain, but she kept going on and trusting God. Accordingly, she continued to get healed. She is strength to me. Like my son and my husband, she uplifts me.

I also think of a friend of mine who suffered from cancer. She has gone on to be with the Lord now, but she was a woman of strength. She continued to hold, trust, and obey. She gave me strength. She taught me how to find strength in my weakness. I think of so many people, especially women in my life who have experienced so much pain––young girls and boys trying to fit in the group, young single moms trying to do it all, young and old women experiencing illnesses, death, divorce, financial stressors, and so much more. And I always come back to thinking of my son continuing his journey on the tennis tour.

We all have to come boldly to him, admitting
our faults and moving on.

"Be of good courage and he shall strengthen your
heart, all ye that hope in the Lord" (Psalm 1:24).

Meet the enemy head on. During December 1999, we were visiting my in-laws for the holidays. Right after Christmas, my son had tournament tennis in Tennessee, and we had to get him to Tampa International Airport by 9:00 A.M. We got up ready to go, but our auto would not crank. There were some hydraulic problems, so we took my father-in-law's car and made the journey to the airport.

It started to rain. Soon we had to drive through hard and rough weather. We were about a half a mile from the airport when we hit a pool of water that spun the car around. Several other cars were coming toward us, and I started shouting the name of Jesus over and over again. We were protected in the name of Jesus. My husband and my son were astonished. They were so amazed that we were not touched. All coming cars stopped. We looked around, and we were back on the interstate headed to the airport.

There again was that strength from my Father. I called on his name, and he protected us. I really believe this was an exercise that opened my husband's and my son's eyes that God is alive, real, and always there. In other words, God is still God. I was amazed at my tactics. I sat in that car praising and thanking God again for favor, grace, and mercy. I acknowledged that he had given us the victory in the name of Jesus.

I realize I have no power of my own.
I must rely on the Holy Spirit's power.

I have discovered that when we operate on faith and not fear, God works it out, big time, and that bad devil is defeated!

How can God use me? What can I do as a woman?

Everyone who asks receives.

And I say unto you, Ask, and it shall be given you; seek, and ye shall find; knock, and it shall be opened unto you. For every one that asketh receiveth; and he that seeketh findeth; and to him that knocketh it shall be opened (Luke 11:9-10).

TESTIMONY FOUR: DARLENE

Darlene was a Proverbs 31 Woman. She was diligent, and her home was warm and loving. It wasn't always tidy, but much warmth and love was in that home. Aunt Darlene was a woman of faith. She was married to Mose. Mose and Darlene never had children of their own, but professed to be mom and dad to all of their great-nieces and great-nephews. Darlene made the home special, and she did toot her own horn. She was not much of a church goer, but she did love God.

She calculated insurance policies and sold and bought property. She owned much acreage in Louisiana (Bayou Parish). Aunt Darlene was a woman who knew what buying and selling was. She had a big house filled with antiques. She was truly a godly, Proverbs 31 Woman. She used her money with lots of faith.

As she grew in her knowledge of the Lord, she gained new character and new ways of handling money. Her stewardship told the story about what she really believed. She was one to often think about and give money to the poor. It reminds me of the Bible story she would share with us, as we would visit her home and go into her large backyard and pick strawberries, blackberries, and figs. She had numerous fig trees.

Now when Jesus heard these things, he said unto him, Yet lackest thou one thing: sell all that thou hast, and distribute unto the poor, and thou shalt have treasure in heaven: and come, follow me (Luke 18:22).

Thou shalt have no other gods before me. Thou shalt not covet thy neighbour's house, thou shalt not covet thy neighbour's wife, nor his manservant, nor his maidservant, nor his ox, nor his ass, nor any thing that is thy neighbour's (Exodus 20:3, 17).

She was not at all like that young man in the Bible, but she used that story to paint the picture of how not to be with your money. Money related to our love of God because there is a relationship between our true spiritual condition and our attitude concerning money and our possessions. Fortunately, Aunt Darlene did not power a wrong or bad attitude towards money. She was not a coveting woman. She was good at obeying God's Word. Darlene was not at all like that rich farmer who had a great crop and didn't know where to put it all.

And he said unto them, Take heed, and beware of covetousness: for a man's life consisteth not in the abundance of the things which he possesseth. And he spake a parable unto them, saying, The ground of a certain rich man brought forth plentifully: And he thought within himself, saying, What shall I do, because I have no room where to bestow my fruits?

And he said, This will I do: I will pull down my barns, and build greater; and there will I bestow all my fruits and my goods. And I will say to my soul, Soul, thou hast much goods laid up for many years; take thine ease, eat, drink, and be merry.

> But God said unto him, Thou fool, this night thy soul shall be required of thee: then whose shall those things be, which thou hast provided? So is he that layeth up treasure for himself, and is not rich toward God (Luke 12:15-21).

Aunt Darlene was a giver. "It's more blessed to give than to receive" (Acts 20:35). She gave of her money, her time, and herself. Darlene gave, and Darlene received. God helped Darlene to be more giving to her family, friends, and other relatives. She was able to bless people in many ways: buying bus tickets, giving good helpings with housing, as well as food, clothing, shelter, and more.

> There is that scattereth, and yet increaseth; and there is that withholdeth more than is meet, but it tendeth to poverty. The liberal soul shall be made fat: and he that watereth shall be watered also himself (Proverbs 11:24-25).

> But this I say, He which soweth sparingly shall reap also sparingly; and he which soweth bountifully shall reap also bountifully (2 Corinthians 9:6).

Darlene's philosophy was: when you let go of money, you let go of part of yourself. When you give money, you release a lot of your ego-self.

> And the multitude of them that believed were of one heart and of one soul: neither said any of them that ought of the things which he possessed was his own; but they had all things common. And with great power gave the apostles witness of the resurrection of the Lord Jesus: and great grace was upon them all.

> Neither was there any among them that lacked: for as many as were possessors of lands or houses sold

them, and brought the prices of the things that were sold, And laid them down at the apostles' feet: and distribution was made unto every man according as he had need.

And Joses, who by the apostles was surnamed Barnabas, (which is, being interpreted, The son of consolation,) a Levite, and of the country of Cyprus, Having land, sold it, and brought the money, and laid it at the apostles' feet (Acts 4:32-37).

"Give, and it will be given to you" (Luke 6:38 NKJV).

*Giving money is an effective way of showing
our love to God because it is a
part of us and reveals what is important to us.*

Giving demonstrates faith.

Faith breaks the spirit of fear that tries to have us believe that we should hold onto our money. Darlene was a woman of faith who did her best to follow God's plan. Darlene possessed much wisdom. She knew Proverbs. She balanced her life and was farsighted. In other words, Darlene kept one eye on the future and the other eye on reality.

Wilt thou set thine eyes upon that which is not? for riches certainly make themselves wings; they fly away as an eagle toward heaven (Proverbs 23:5).

Cease, my son, to hear the instruction that causeth to err from the words of knowledge (Proverbs 19:27).

Much food is in the tillage of the poor: but there is that is destroyed for want of judgment (Proverbs 13:23).

Darlene had faith. We must all keep in mind that faith is sufficient. The first thing I must know is to have faith.

> I beseech you therefore, brethren, by the mercies of God, that ye present your bodies a living sacrifice, holy, acceptable unto God, which is your reasonable service. And be not conformed to this world: but be ye transformed by the renewing of your mind, that ye may prove what is that good, and acceptable, and perfect, will of God. For I say, through the grace given unto me, to every man that is among you, not to think of himself more highly than he ought to think; but to think soberly, according as God hath dealt to every man the measure of faith.
>
> For as we have many members in one body, and all members have not the same office: So we, being many, are one body in Christ, and every one members one of another. Having then gifts differing according to the grace that is given to us, whether prophecy, let us prophesy according to the proportion of faith; Or ministry, let us wait on our ministering: or he that teacheth, on teaching; Or he that exhorteth, on exhortation: he that giveth, let him do it with simplicity; he that ruleth, with diligence; he that sheweth mercy, with cheerfulness.
>
> Let love be without dissimulation. Abhor that which is evil; cleave to that which is good. Be kindly affectioned one to another with brotherly love; in honour preferring one another; Not slothful in business; fervent in spirit; serving the Lord; Rejoicing in hope; patient in tribulation; continuing instant in prayer; Distributing to the necessity of saints; given to hospitality.

Bless them which persecute you: bless, and curse not. Rejoice with them that do rejoice, and weep with them that weep. Be of the same mind one toward another. Mind not high things, but condescend to men of low estate. Be not wise in your own conceits. Recompense to no man evil for evil. Provide things honest in the sight of all men.

If it be possible, as much as lieth in you, live peaceably with all men. Dearly beloved, avenge not yourselves, but rather give place unto wrath: for it is written, Vengeance is mine; I will repay, saith the Lord. Therefore if thine enemy hunger, feed him; if he thirst, give him drink: for in so doing thou shalt heap coals of fire on his head. Be not overcome of evil, but overcome evil with good (Romans 12).

Promise Four

TO EMBRACE YOUR WORD LIKE GUIDING STARS

These are additional scriptures on faith that shine upon us like guiding stars, especially relating to our *faith in the true God*.

> *Thou shalt have no other gods before me. Thou shalt not make unto thee any graven image, or any likeness of any thing that is in heaven above, or that is in the earth beneath, or that is in the water under the earth:*

> *Thou shalt not bow down thyself to them, nor serve them: for I the LORD thy God am a jealous God, visiting the iniquity of the fathers upon the children unto the third and fourth generation of them that hate me; And shewing mercy unto thousands of them that love me, and keep my commandments (Exodus 20:3-6).*

> *Thou shalt have none other gods before me. Thou shalt not make thee any graven image, or any likeness of any thing that is in heaven above, or that is in the*

earth beneath, or that is in the waters beneath the earth: Thou shalt not bow down thyself unto them, nor serve them: for I the LORD thy God am a jealous God, visiting the iniquity of the fathers upon the children unto the third and fourth generation of them that hate me, And shewing mercy unto thousands of them that love me and keep my commandments (Deuteronomy 5: 7-10).

Hear, O Israel: The LORD our God is one LORD: And thou shalt love the LORD thy God with all thine heart, and with all thy soul, and with all thy might.

And these words, which I command thee this day, shall be in thine heart: And thou shalt teach them diligently unto thy children, and shalt talk of them when thou sittest in thine house, and when thou walkest by the way, and when thou liest down, and when thou risest up. And thou shalt bind them for a sign upon thine hand, and they shall be as frontlets between thine eyes. And thou shalt write them upon the posts of thy house, and on thy gates.

And it shall be, when the LORD thy God shall have brought thee into the land which he sware unto thy fathers, to Abraham, to Isaac, and to Jacob, to give thee great and goodly cities, which thou buildedst not, And houses full of all good things, which thou filledst not, and wells digged, which thou diggedst not, vineyards and olive trees, which thou plantedst not; when thou shalt have eaten and be full; Then beware lest thou forget the LORD, which brought thee forth out of the land of Egypt, from the house of bondage.

Thou shalt fear the LORD thy God, and serve him, and shalt swear by his name. Ye shall not go after other gods, of the gods of the people which are round about you; (For the LORD thy God is a jealous God among you) lest the anger of the LORD thy God be kindled against thee, and destroy thee from off the face of the earth (Deuteronomy 6:4-15).

Blessed is the man that trusteth in the LORD, and whose hope the LORD is. For he shall be as a tree planted by the waters, and that spreadeth out her roots by the river, and shall not see when heat cometh, but her leaf shall be green; and shall not be careful in the year of drought, neither shall cease from yielding fruit (Jeremiah 17:7-8).

Then said Jesus unto his disciples, If any man will come after me, let him deny himself, and take up his cross, and follow me. For whosoever will save his life shall lose it: and whosoever will lose his life for my sake shall find it.

For what is a man profited, if he shall gain the whole world, and lose his own soul? or what shall a man give in exchange for his soul? For the Son of man shall come in the glory of his Father with his angels; and then he shall reward every man according to his works (Matthew 16:24-27).

Jesus said unto him, If thou canst believe, all things are possible to him that believeth (Mark 9:23).

Also I say unto you, Whosoever shall confess me before men, him shall the Son of man also confess before the angels of God (Luke 12:8).

For God so loved the world, that he gave his only begotten Son, that whosoever believeth in him should not perish, but have everlasting life. He that believeth on the Son hath everlasting life: and he that believeth not the Son shall not see life; but the wrath of God abideth on him (John 3:16, 36).

Verily, verily, I say unto you, He that heareth my word, and believeth on him that sent me, hath everlasting life, and shall not come into condemnation; but is passed from death unto life (John 5:24).

I am come a light into the world, that whosoever believeth on me should not abide in darkness (John 12:46).

In the beginning was the Word, and the Word was with God, and the Word was God. The same was in the beginning with God. All things were made by him; and without him was not any thing made that was made. In him was life; and the life was the light of men.

But as many as received him, to them gave he power to become the sons of God, even to them that believe on his name: Which were born, not of blood, nor of the will of the flesh, nor of the will of man, but of God. And the Word was made flesh, and dwelt among us, (and we beheld his glory, the glory as of the only begotten of the Father,) full of grace and truth (John 14:1-4, 12-14).

And this is life eternal, that they might know thee the only true God, and Jesus Christ, whom thou hast sent (John 17:3).

But Thomas, one of the twelve, called Didymus, was not with them when Jesus came. The other disciples therefore said unto him, We have seen the Lord. But he said unto them, Except I shall see in his hands the print of the nails, and put my finger into the print of the nails, and thrust my hand into his side, I will not believe.

And after eight days again his disciples were within, and Thomas with them: then came Jesus, the doors being shut, and stood in the midst, and said, Peace be unto you. Then saith he to Thomas, Reach hither thy finger, and behold my hands; and reach hither thy hand, and thrust it into my side: and be not faithless, but believing.

And Thomas answered and said unto him, My Lord and my God. Jesus saith unto him, Thomas, because thou hast seen me, thou hast believed: blessed are they that have not seen, and yet have believed. And many other signs truly did Jesus in the presence of his disciples, which are not written in this book: But these are written, that ye might believe that Jesus is the Christ, the Son of God; and that believing ye might have life through his name (John 20:24-31).

To him give all the prophets witness, that through his name whosoever believeth in him shall receive remission of sins (Acts 10:43).

And they said, Believe on the Lord Jesus Christ, and thou shalt be saved, and thy house (Acts 16:31).

For what saith the scripture? Abraham believed God, and it was counted unto him for righteousness. Now to him that worketh is the reward not reckoned of grace, but of debt But to him that worketh not, but believeth on him that justifieth the ungodly, his faith is counted for righteousness.

Even as David also describeth the blessedness of the man, unto whom God imputeth righteousness without works, Saying, Blessed are they whose iniquities are forgiven, and whose sins are covered. Blessed is the man to whom the Lord will not impute sin (Romans 4:3-8).

That if thou shalt confess with thy mouth the Lord Jesus, and shalt believe in thine heart that God hath raised him from the dead, thou shalt be saved. For with the heart man believeth unto righteousness; and with the mouth confession is made unto salvation. For the scripture saith, Whosoever believeth on him shall not be ashamed.

For there is no difference between the Jew and the Greek: for the same Lord over all is rich unto all that call upon him. For whosoever shall call upon the name of the Lord shall be saved (Romans 10:9-13).

Are ye so foolish? having begun in the Spirit, are ye now made perfect by the flesh? Have ye suffered so many things in vain? if it be yet in vain. He therefore that ministereth to you the Spirit, and worketh miracles among you, doeth he it by the works of the law, or by the hearing of faith?

Even as Abraham believed God, and it was accounted to him for righteousness. Know ye therefore that they which are of faith, the same are the children *of Abraham. And the scripture, foreseeing that God would justify the heathen through faith, preached before the gospel unto Abraham, saying, In thee shall all nations be blessed. So then they which be of faith are blessed with faithful Abraham.*

Christ hath redeemed us from the curse of the law, being made a curse for us: for it is written, Cursed is every one that hangeth on a tree: That the blessing of Abraham might come on the Gentiles through Jesus Christ; that we might receive the promise of the Spirit through faith. (Galatians 3:6-9, 13-14).

Now faith is the substance of things hoped for, the evidence of things not seen. For by it the elders obtained a good report. Through faith we understand that the worlds were framed by the word of God, so that things which are seen were not made of things which do appear.

By faith Abel offered unto God a more excellent sacrifice than Cain, by which he obtained witness that he was righteous, God testifying of his gifts: and by it he being dead yet speaketh.

By faith Enoch was translated that he should not see death; and was not found, because God had translated him: for before his translation he had this testimony, that he pleased God. But without faith it is impossible to please him: for he that cometh to God must believe that he is, and that he is a rewarder of them that diligently seek him.

By faith Noah, being warned of God of things not seen as yet, moved with fear, prepared an ark to the saving of his house; by the which he condemned the world, and became heir of the righteousness which is by faith.

By faith Abraham, when he was called to go out into a place which he should after receive for an inheritance, obeyed; and he went out, not knowing whither he went. By faith he sojourned in the land of promise, as in a strange country, dwelling in tabernacles with Isaac and Jacob, the heirs with him of the same promise: For he looked for a city which hath foundations, whose builder and maker is God.

Through faith also Sara herself received strength to conceive seed, and was delivered of a child when she was past age, because she judged him faithful who had promised. Therefore sprang there even of one, and him as good as dead, so many as the stars of the sky in multitude, and as the sand which is by the sea shore innumerable.

These all died in faith, not having received the promises, but having seen them afar off, and were persuaded of them, and embraced them, and confessed that they were strangers and pilgrims on the earth. For they that say such things declare plainly that they seek a country. And truly, if they had been mindful of that country from whence they came out, they might have had opportunity to have returned. But now they desire a better country, that is, an heavenly: wherefore God is not ashamed to be called their God: for he hath prepared for them a city.

By faith Abraham, when he was tried, offered up Isaac: and he that had received the promises offered up his only begotten son, Of whom it was said, That in Isaac shall thy seed be called: Accounting that God was able to raise him up, even from the dead; from whence also he received him in a figure.

By faith Isaac blessed Jacob and Esau concerning things to come.

By faith Jacob, when he was a dying, blessed both the sons of Joseph; and worshipped, leaning upon the top of his staff.

By faith Joseph, when he died, made mention of the departing of the children of Israel; and gave commandment concerning his bones.

By faith Moses, when he was born, was hid three months of his parents, because they saw he was a proper child; and they were not afraid of the king's commandment. By faith Moses, when he was come to years, refused to be called the son of Pharaoh's daughter; Choosing rather to suffer affliction with the people of God, than to enjoy the pleasures of sin for a season; Esteeming the reproach of Christ greater riches than the treasures in Egypt: for he had respect unto the recompence of the reward. By faith he forsook Egypt, not fearing the wrath of the king: for he endured, as seeing him who is invisible.

Through faith he kept the passover, and the sprinkling of blood, lest he that destroyed the firstborn should touch them. By faith they passed through the Red sea as by dry land: which the Egyptians assaying to do were drowned. By faith the walls of Jericho fell down, after they were compassed about seven days.

By faith the harlot Rahab perished not with them that believed not, when she had received the spies with peace.

And what shall I more say? for the time would fail me to tell of Gedeon, and of Barak, and of Samson, and of Jephthae; of David also, and Samuel, and of the prophets: Who through faith subdued kingdoms, wrought righteousness, obtained promises, stopped the mouths of lions, Quenched the violence of fire, escaped the edge of the sword, out of weakness were made strong, waxed valiant in fight, turned to flight the armies of the aliens. Women received their dead raised to life again: and others were tortured, not accepting deliverance; that they might obtain a better resurrection: And others had trial of cruel mockings and scourgings, yea, moreover of bonds and imprisonment: They were stoned, they were sawn asunder, were tempted, were slain with the sword: they wandered about in sheepskins and goatskins; being destitute, afflicted, tormented; (Of whom the world was not worthy:) they wandered in deserts, and in mountains, and in dens and caves of the earth.

And these all, having obtained a good report through faith, received not the promise: God having provided some better thing for us, that they without us should not be made perfect.

Wherefore seeing we also are compassed about with so great a cloud of witnesses, let us lay aside every weight, and the sin which doth so easily beset us, and let us run with patience the race that is set before us, Looking unto Jesus the author and finisher of our faith; who for the joy that was set before him endured the cross, despising the shame, and is set down at the right hand of the throne of God. For consider him that endured such contradiction of sinners against himself, lest ye be wearied and faint in your minds (Hebrews 11:1-12:3).

Blessed be the God and Father of our Lord Jesus Christ, which according to his abundant mercy hath begotten us again unto a lively hope by the resurrection of Jesus Christ from the dead, To an inheritance incorruptible, and undefiled, and that fadeth not away, reserved in heaven for you, Who are kept by the power of God through faith unto salvation ready to be revealed in the last time.

Wherein ye greatly rejoice, though now for a season, if need be, ye are in heaviness through manifold temptations: That the trial of your faith, being much more precious than of gold that perisheth, though it be tried with fire, might be found unto praise and honour and glory at the appearing of Jesus Christ: Whom having not seen, ye love; in whom, though now ye see him not, yet believing, ye rejoice with joy unspeakable and full of glory: (1 Peter 1:3-9).

Let that therefore abide in you, which ye have heard from the beginning. If that which ye have heard from the beginning shall remain in you, ye also shall continue in the Son, and in the Father. And this is the promise that he hath promised us, even eternal life (1 John 2:24-25).

After this I beheld, and, lo, a great multitude, which no man could number, of all nations, and kindreds, and people, and tongues, stood before the throne, and before the Lamb, clothed with white robes, and palms in their hands;

And one of the elders answered, saying unto me, What are these which are arrayed in white robes? and whence came they? And I said unto him, Sir, thou knowest. And he said to me, These are they which came out of great tribulation, and have washed their robes, and made them white in the blood of the Lamb. Therefore are they before the throne of God, and serve him day and night in his temple: and he that sitteth on the throne shall dwell among them. They shall hunger no more, neither thirst any more; neither shall the sun light on them, nor any heat.

For the Lamb which is in the midst of the throne shall feed them, and shall lead them unto living fountains of waters: and God shall wipe away all tears from their eyes (Revelation 7:9, 13-17).

And I saw a new heaven and a new earth: for the first heaven and the first earth were passed away; and there was no more sea. And I John saw the holy city, new Jerusalem, coming down from God out of heaven, prepared as a bride adorned for her husband.

And I heard a great voice out of heaven saying, Behold, the tabernacle of God is with men, and he will dwell with them, and they shall be his people, and God himself shall be with them, and be their God. And God shall wipe away all tears from their eyes; and there shall be no more death, neither sorrow, nor crying, neither shall there be any more pain: for the former things are passed away.

And he that sat upon the throne said, Behold, I make all things new. And he said unto me, Write: for these words are true and faithful. And he said unto me, It is done. I am Alpha and Omega, the beginning and the end. I will give unto him that is athirst of the fountain of the water of life freely. He that overcometh shall inherit all things; and I will be his God, and he shall be my son (Revelation 21:1-7).

And he shewed me a pure river of water of life, clear as crystal, proceeding out of the throne of God and of the Lamb. In the midst of the street of it, and on either side of the river, was there the tree of life, which bare twelve manner of fruits, and yielded her fruit every month: and the leaves of the tree were for the healing of the nations.

And there shall be no more curse: but the throne of God and of the Lamb shall be in it; and his servants shall serve him: And they shall see his face; and his name shall be in their foreheads. And there shall be no night there; and they need no candle, neither light of the sun; for the Lord God giveth them light: and they shall reign for ever and ever (Revelation 22:1-5, 12-14).

Dear Lord, let these scriptures be read, enjoyed,
and shine into our hearts, creating a pattern
of what we should be:
much like your stars reflect constellations guiding the lost.

Promise Five

TO EMBRACE YOUR SONGS
LIKE GUIDING STARS

The women of faith I have referenced herein did a lot of singing and praising God. Here are just a few of their favorite songs to share with you if you are one to sing as you pray, sing as you work, sing in the shower, or wherever. These are hymns for you to try. They inspired these godly women whose testimonies you have read.

> *And Lord, let these hymns ring in our ears, hearts*
> *and souls to star in and guide our lives.*

"What a Friend We Have in Jesus"

"How Great Thou Art"

"O, for a Thousand Tongues to Sing"

"Great is Thy Faithfulness"

"Holy, Holy, Holy! Lord God Almighty"

"Teach Me to Pray, Lord"

"Rock of Ages, Cleft for Me"

"Breathe on Me, Breath of God"

"My Hope is in the Lord"

"Just as I Am, Without One Plea"

"At the Cross"

"Guide Me, O Thou Great Jehovah"

"Praise to the Lord, the Almighty"

"Fairest Lord Jesus"

"It is Well With my Soul"

"Great is the Lord"

"This is the Day"

"He's Got the Whole World in His Hands"

"I've Got Peace Like a River"

"Rejoice in the Lord Always"

"Amazing Grace"

"There is Power in the Name of Jesus"

"This Little Light of Mine"

"Do Lord"

"I Love You, Lord"

"Father, I Stretch My Hands to Thee"

"Going to Heaven to Meet the King"

"I Will Bless the Lord"

"I Shall Wear a Crown"

"Can't Say Thank You Enough"

"Midnight Cry"

"Sheltered in the Arms of God"

"Breathe, Send Your Rain"

"O Magnify the Lord with Me"

"His Blood Washes Me"

Bonus

IN GRATITUDE, A PRELUDE
TO KIKI'S RECIPES

The members of the Thomas Family convey our gratitude to you for your support as we endured the loss of our wife, mother, grandmother, sister, aunt, and niece. Your love and support have made our loss less painful.

To show our appreciation, we are enclosing something that Kiki treasured. It is also something about which many of you have inquired: the recipe and secret of Kiki's Gumbo. Although some of you may have seen the recipe in an article in *The Atlanta Constitution*, we are presenting the article and recipe as a keepsake.

As you review the article and use it to make gumbo, we also give to you some of Kiki's Gumbo stories. Gumbo is fun, laughter, joy, and love.

<u>Rainy night at the top of First National Bank Tower</u>

Yours truly shared an office with Marvin Arrington, a college and law school mate. As we worked on a cold and rainy night, Marvin said that the night was a perfect night for gumbo. He asked if we had some at home. I responded that we did not, as I had eaten the last of the batch days earlier. Marvin, being Marvin, secretly called Kiki and told her that I asked him to call and requested that she make some gumbo for us. I only knew what Marvin had done after he came into my office laughing uncontrollably. When I inquired as to why he was laughing, he said, "Kiki said to tell you that on this rainy, cold night, neither of your wishes would come true tonight!"

The Preacher and the Gumbo

Kiki was known for coming and delivering gumbo to friends. Sometimes she would call and tell her friends to stop by and get some. She also used it for reward and punishment with me. Such was the case a few years ago. After retiring, Kiki developed a love for cooking. Sometimes she would begin cooking gumbo in the morning before I departed for work.

One morning she had laid out the jumbo shrimp, crabs, and fresh vegetables (all the ingredients that I liked.) Because I had seen the ingredients before left, I was able to smell and taste the gumbo throughout the day. However, during the course of the day, a conflict arose, and she became angry with me. The anger exceeded her level of kindness and matrimony. Little did I realize how angry she was until I arrived home. I sensed the smell of fresh cooked gumbo throughout the house, but there was no gumbo on the stove, table, refrigerator, or freezer. As the outside temperature was below 30, I even looked outside. But to my surprise, there was no gumbo. When I inquired about the gumbo, her response was she had taken it to Rev. Dr. Joseph Lowery and left it at his door as he was not home. She said that he deserved it and I did not. When I inquired as to why she did not leave a bowl, she said that she thought about leaving some for me. But after she became angry with me, she put okra in it. (I do not eat okra.) She said that I did not even deserve okra-filled gumbo.

The Gumbo in New York

O. T. Wells is a good friend who loved Kiki's gumbo. O. T. was so in love with the gumbo that he requested that Kiki travel to New York for his 75th birthday and prepare gumbo. In order to comply with this request, O. T. convinced his friend, Regina Darby of New York, to turn over her kitchen to Kiki for Kiki to prepare a gumbo. Kiki complied. Kiki threw down the ladle! Everyone loved it, and O. T. was happy.

The Gumbo at Atlanta Airport

Kiki celebrated her 65th birthday on February 15, 2012. She wanted a 65th birthday party. Kiki's college friend and she agreed that they would have a lavish 65th birthday party. To show his affection for Kiki, O. T. Wells delivered 64 long stemmed yellow roses with one long stemmed red rose. Kiki prepared some gumbo for their celebration. Before leaving Atlanta, O. T. requested that Kiki prepare some gumbo for him to take to New York. Kiki obliged and prepared a container for O. T.'s travel. In so doing, no one considered security and how this container with liquid would get past security. When O. T. arrived at security, the container was rejected. O. T. was given the choice of returning it to Kiki or discarding it. O. T., being the great lawyer that he is, argued to security that the gumbo was too good to be returned or discarded. In support of his argument, O. T. opened the container and allowed some of the aroma to fill the air. O. T. proposed rather than discarding or returning the gumbo that he would get several spoons and that he and security personnel eat the gumbo at the check point. O. T. prevailed and was allowed to board the plane with his gumbo.

Gumbo and Basketball

Kiantki played basketball and ice hockey before deciding to concentrate exclusively on tennis. As a basketball player, the team played a holiday tournament at a school in East Point, Georgia. As our house is in East Point and three miles from the place of the tournament, Kiki decided to provide dinner for the team, coaches, and parents. She finished the gumbo about noon and permitted me to taste it. It was good, and I said that it would be great that night after it aged. Before leaving for the game that evening I decided to have a bowl. To my surprise the gumbo had aged too much and had become spoiled. It spoiled because Kiki put oysters in it and it was not properly refrigerated. Kiki was determined that the invitees would have gumbo. She did not go to the game, but shopped for the necessary ingredients and made it available for the players, coaches, and family members after the game. The gumbo served was not as good as the gumbo which had aged too much.

Gumbo and Food Poison

Interestingly Kiki's love for gumbo almost led to her death. During Mardi Gras in 2014 Kiki accompanied Kiantki, Valentina, Issiah, and Moses to Louisiana to visit Mama Rosie, as Valentia and the kids had never visited Plaquemine, Louisiana. During the stay, a visit was made to a particular restaurant. Kiki had gumbo which contained oysters. She loved to eat gumbo at different places for comparison purposes. No one else in her party had gumbo. Upon returning to the hotel, Kiki became very ill to the degree that medics rushed her to the hospital the next morning. Kiki remained hospitalized for two days. After two days of tests and evaluation, it was determined that she had suffered food poison. The culprit was gumbo. Needless to say, a claim was filed, and when the restaurant refused to compensate her, a lawsuit was filed. Kiki prevailed and received a judgment.

Gumbo and Red Beans and Rice

During the fall of 1970 Kiki's mother came to visit her in Atlanta. During the time of the visit Kiki and I were very much involved, but her mother was not pleased at the direction and pace of the relationship. Mama Rosie was of the opinion that we had dated long enough that marriage should be a part of my plans. Mama Rosie suggested that we discuss the matter over dinner which she would prepare at Kiki's place. I agreed to come to dinner but advised her that I did not eat pork. Mama Rosie said that she would prepare the foods that were served at Mary's Place, the family restaurant in Plaquemine. The meal consisted of fried chicken, red beans and rice and gumbo. It was delicious. Mama Rosie let me know that if I were to come to Plaquemine for Thanksgiving, I would be fed in the same manner. It was only when I came to Plaquemine that I learned the nature of the meal which was prepared in Atlanta. Kiki's brothers and cousins told me that red beans and rice was considered to be an aphrodisiac. They advised me that they never ate red beans and rice at a woman's house and that I should have refused their mother's and aunt's red beans and rice. I asked about the gumbo and told them that gumbo was debatable.

Publication of Gumbo Recipes

As president of the Gate City Barristers Wives, Kiki led the group in the publication of a cookbook. In the book, the wives presented their favorite recipes. Kiki's recipe was also published in *The Atlanta Constitution* where she was featured in the paper's Thursday Food Section. It appears that anytime a gumbo recipe is published, it is subjected to harsh criticism. One of the ladies was subjected to a heavy critique because she said that she puts wieners in her gumbo. Kiki was criticized because she includes tomatoes in her gumbo. Kiki always had a response to the questions regarding the ingredients: "It's gumbo!"

There are many more stories surrounding Kiki and her gumbo; these are only a few! The term "gumbo" is used because, like fine wine, Kiki's gumbos were never the same level of goodness. They were always good; sometimes they were even great! Commenting on her own gumbo, she would say sometimes that it was the ingredients, and sometimes it was the season. Sometimes it was the utensil (five-gallon aluminum pot, cast iron pot, manganite pots, or wooden spoons.) However, I am of the opinion that love is the main ingredient for great gumbo. When she made gumbo on days when she was filled with joy and laughter; on days which she danced and sang; on days when she prayed enthusiastically, the gumbo was great.

Therefore, please keep this in mind: even though you have the recipes, remember that unless you make it with love and love making it, it may be good, but it will not be great.

Bon Appetit!

Love and peace,
Antonio Thomas, Esq.

Promise Six

TO LOVE YOUR GIFTS OF BODY, HEART, AND TASTE

Wonderful recipes of Ma Mary and others.

Cinnamon Bread

¼ lb. butter
2 C. flour
3 t. baking powder
½ and ⅓ C. sugar
¾ milk
1 T. cinnamon
2 eggs at room temperature
½ t. salt

Melt butter and cool to lukewarm. In another bowl, sift together two cups of flour, baking powder, and salt. Beat 2 eggs until very thick. Beat in ½ cup of sugar, a little at a time. Beat ¼ cup of the melted butter. Add the dry ingredients alternately with the milk, beginning and ending with the dry ingredients. Place in the loaf pan, an 8 ½ X

4 ½ X 3 inch, which has been greased on the bottom. Blend together ⅓ cup of sugar and 1 T cinnamon. Sprinkle over batter. Pour the rest of the butter over the top. Cut through the batter serval times with a knife. Bake for 40 minutes until bread starts to shrink from the sides of the pan. Bake at 350 degrees. Let stand for 10 minutes and then cool on a cake rack.

Mama Adleane's
Pumpkin Bread

1 16 oz. can of pumpkin
3 ½ cups self-rising flour
2 teaspoons of baking soda
3 cups sugar
1 ½ teaspoons salt
1 teaspoon cinnamon
1 teaspoon nutmeg
1 cup oil
⅔ cup water
4 eggs
½ cup of pecans or walnuts

Sift dry ingredients. Make a well in the bowl of dry ingredients and add the following:

Oil, water, pumpkin, and eggs. Mix until smooth. Pour into two or three greased and floured

loaf pans; bake for one hour at 350 degrees.

Adleane's Louisiana
The Most Basic Yeast Bread Recipe
To Make ONE loaf, you will need:

4 ½ cups of flour
1 package of yeast

2 tablespoons of sugar
1 teaspoon of salt
1 cup of very warm water (120 to 130 degrees F.)
2 tablespoons of oil
1 large bowl
1 large strong spoon
A bread board or a clean, flat surface
Clean hands

This is what you do:

Into a large bowl, mix the following:

1 ¼ cups of flour
1 package of yeast
2 tablespoons of sugar
1 teaspoon salt

Add:

1 cup of very warm water (too hot will kill the yeast)
2 tablespoons of oil

Now use your spoon to stir the mixture. Stir for about 100 strokes (or use an electric mixer at medium speed for about three minutes.) While you stir with your spoon (don't use the mixer, it may burn up its motor), gradually add:

2 cups of flour

When dough has taken up all of this flour, gradually add:

More flour (probably less than a cup) until the dough is smooth, pliable, and no longer sticky. Be careful not to add too much flour; do it in small amounts.

Now move the dough to the bread board and knead the dough for five minutes or more. (The longer, the better.) Place the dough in a greased bread pan. Cover, place the pan in a warm place, free of drafts. Let it rise for 45 minutes.

You can bake it now or let it rise a second time. I think that it is better to let it rise twice, but if you don't have time, go on to the next step. (If you let it rise twice, punch the dough down, re-cover it and let it rise again 30 minutes.)

Remove the cover from the dough. Be careful to do it gently or you will make the loaf go flat.

Place the loaf in a pre-heated oven set for 375 degrees F. Bake the loaf for about 30-minutes. Test the loaf. Does it sound hollow when you tap it? If you stick a clean knife into the bottom of the loaf, does it come out free of dough? (There will be water on the knife). Both answers should be yes! If not, the loaf is not done. Place it back into the oven for five minutes, then re-test it. Let it cool, then eat.

Thank you, Lord, for

Aunt Betty's
Cheese Pancakes

2 C. cottage cheese. Sieved (I blend it until it is smooth in blender.)
2 eggs
¼ t salt
butter
2 T. honey
½ C. whole wheat flour

Beat eggs, salt, honey and flour into cottage cheese. Melt some butter in a large skillet. Drop the batter by rounded tsp into the hot skillet. Add butter as needed. Keep pancakes small. These are good with preserves or maple syrup.

Aunt Darlene's Louisiana
Corn Fritters

1 C. corn (fresh, frozen, or canned)
1 egg
½ Tsp. salt
½ Tsp. baking powder
¼ C. mill
¼ C. flour

Mix ingredients. Drop batter by spoonfuls into skillet containing ½ inch hot oil. Fry until golden brown on both sides.

Dear God, appreciation to You for

Aunt Stella's
French Toast

2 slightly beaten eggs
½ C. milk
1 tablespoon sugar
6 thick (1-inch) slices of bread
butter or margarine – dash cinnamon

Combine eggs, milk, sugar, and cinnamon. Dip bread slices into egg mixture to coat evenly. Grill on hot skillet in butter until brown on both sides.

Louisiana Mama Mary
Angel Biscuits

1 pk. Yeast
2-3 T. warm water
5 cups flour
3-5 t. sugar
1 T. baking powder

1 t. salt
1 t. baking soda
1 C. Crisco
2 C. buttermilk

Dissolve yeast in warm water. Sift together dry ingredients. Cut in Crisco. Add buttermilk and yeast together to dry ingredient mixture.

Knead dough, roll out, and cut into biscuits. Bake at 400 degrees for about 25 minutes or until biscuits are brown.

There is so much to thank you for, Oh, Lord! Now we are ready to savor.

Plaquemine's Easy Biscuits

2 C. self-rising flour
4 T. mayonnaise
1 C. milk

Mix ingredients and drop batter into well-greased muffin pans, filling ⅓ full. Bake at 450 degrees for 10 minutes.

Honey Buns

⅔ C. butter
⅔ C. honey
½ C. sugar
½ C. chopped nuts
2 pkg. refrigerated biscuits

Melt butter in a 9 x 13-inch pan. Stir in honey and sugar, bring to boiling on medium heat. Boil one minute, stirring constantly. Sprinkle with nuts. Place biscuits over honey mixture. Bake at 425 degrees for 12 minutes. Turn upside down to serve.

Mama Adleane's
Quick Dinner Rolls

1 pkg. active dry yeast
1 ½ C. flour

2 T. shortening
1 t. salt
2 T. sugar
1 egg
1 C. of flour

Dissolve yeast in one cup of warm water. Then add 1 ½ cups flour, shortening, salt, sugar, and egg. Mix well. Gradually add last cup of flour. Let rise for 45 minutes. Press down and into muffin cups. Let rise again for 30 minutes. Bake 15 minutes at 350 degrees.

And now, Sweet Lord, we have

Banana Oatmeal Muffins

½ C. uncooked oats, quick or regular
½ C. milk
1 C. unsifted all-purpose flour
¼ C. sugar
2 ½ t. baking powder
½ t. baking soda
½ t. salt
½ t. cinnamon
¼ t. nutmeg
¼ C. butter or margarine, melted
1 egg
1 C. mashed ripe bananas (3 medium

In medium bowl, combine oats and milk; set aside until milk is absorbed. In medium bowl, mix flour, sugar, baking powder, baking soda, salt, cinnamon and nutmeg. Add butter, egg and bananas to oat mixture; add to dry ingredients and stir just until moistened. Fill greased 2 ½ inch muffin cups ⅔ full. Bake at 425 degrees in oven for 15 minutes or until cake tester inserted in center comes out clean. Yield: 12-14 muffins.

Yet another gift from God is

Aunt Stella's Melon Dip

1 carton sour cream
⅓ C. sweetened condensed milk
½ carton refrigerated dessert topping
Cinnamon
Nutmeg
Bowl of melon balls

Mix all ingredients thoroughly; pour over melon balls or dip individually.

For a mixed fruit bowl, prepare the following:
1 cup fresh pineapple chunks
1 cup strawberries
1 cup seedless green grapes
1 cup watermelon balls
1 cup honeydew balls
1 cup cantaloupe balls
1 cup sliced bananas

God never stops blessing us. Amen and
we give him praise and honor.

Mama's Fried Sweet Potatoes

Peel raw, sweet potatoes and cut them in slices. Place them in hot fat and when they are slightly brown turn them. Keep the skillet covered as the steam cooks the potato slices. When lightly browned or apparently tender, sprinkle with sugar and add about two tablespoons of hot water. Put on the lid and allow them to cook about two minutes longer.

Mama Adleane's
Glazed Carrots

3-4 C. diagonally sliced carrots
1 C. orange juice
½ C. chicken broth
3 cloves
¼ t. ginger
1 ½ T. lemon rind

Mix together all the above ingredients and bring to a boil. Add in three teaspoons sugar.

Simmer half hour or until carrots are tender.

Mama Adleane's
Rice with Zucchini

1 small zucchini, about ½ pound
3 T. butter
⅓ C. finely chopped onion
1 C. rice
1 ½ C. chicken broth
Salt and pepper to taste, if desired

Trim the ends of the zucchini. Cut the zucchini into half-inch cubes. There should be about one cup.

Heat two tablespoons of the butter in a saucepan and add the onion. Cook, stirring until wilted. Add the zucchini and stir. Add the rice, chicken broth, salt, and pepper.

Bring to a boil. Cover closely and let simmer 17 minutes. Gently stir in the remaining butter and serve.

Mama Adleane's Louisiana Squash Supreme

2 1-lb. frozen, fresh, or canned squash
1 2-oz. jar chopped pimento, drained
2 T. grated onion
2 carrots, grated
1 C. sour cream
1 10 ½ oz. can cream of broth, undiluted
1 8 oz. package herb seasoned stuffing
½ C. melted butter

Combine vegetables; blend sour cream and soup and stir into vegetables. Toss together stuffing and butter. Place half the stuffing in greased shallow 3-quart baking dish. Pour vegetable mixture over layer, then top with remaining stuffing.

Bake at 375 degrees for about 30 minutes.

Makes 8 to 10 servings.

Mama Adleane's Baked Apricots or Apples

1 C. of crackers, crushed
¾ stick butter (approximately)
½ C. brown sugar (firmly packed)
2- 17 oz. unpeeled apricot halves, drained

Place a layer of apricots and or apples sprinkled with sugar, then cracker crumbs dotted with butter (repeat) in a greased casserole dish. Bake at 300 degrees in a preheated oven for one hour. This recipe is used as a vegetable dish. Serves eight.

Mama Adleane's
Crab-Shrimp Casserole

1 green pepper	1 C. mayonnaise
1 medium onion	1 t. Worcestershire sauce
1 C. celery	1 ½ C. of breadcrumbs
1 ½ lbs. crabmeat	3 t. butter or margarine
1 ½ lbs. shrimp	Dash of salt and pepper

Mix all ingredients except breadcrumbs and butter. Put in ungreased baking dish. Melt butter or margarine and toss with breadcrumbs. Sprinkle on top of other ingredients. Bake at 350 degrees for 45-50 minutes.

Mama Adleane, Darlene, Stella, Mary and Betty
all had pieces of this 1# GUMBO FILE

Gumbo File

1 large chicken or the lean meat of a baked chicken or turkey	2 C. shrimp
2 large onions	4 springs parsley
2 T. File powder	1 sprig thyme leaf
2 to 3 dozen oysters	1 C. celery leaves
Salt and pepper to taste	1 bay leaf
1 C. fresh, frozen, or canned tomatoes	1 clove garlic

Several red pepper pods

Clean and cut chicken and sprinkle with salt and pepper. Sauté onion, garlic, celery and chicken until brown. Crush bay leaf and thyme and add chicken with diced shrimp. Sauté for 15 minutes, stirring frequently to prevent burning. When brown, add oyster, juice, and boiling water to cover two inches above ingredients. Add pepper pods, tomatoes, and parsley. Cover and cook at low heat for one hour until done. Add oysters one half hour before serving and cook five minutes. Remove from heat and add File powder. Serve over rice.

Once File is added, gumbo should not be re-warmed. Some people prefer adding File powder to rice. It's only a matter of choice. Allow two or three tablespoons of rice per serving.

Nanna Beth Betty's Favorite Shrimp Kabobs

1 large green pepper, cut into 1-inch pieces
1 (8 oz.) can pineapple chucks in unsweetened juice
¼ C. prepared mustard
1 T. brown sugar
1 lb. fresh, medium shrimp, peeled and deveined
4 slices bacon, cut into thirds
1 (4 oz.) can button mushrooms, drained

Pour boiling water over green pepper pieces; let stand five minutes; drain. Drain pineapple-reserving juice. Combine pineapple juice, mustard, and sugar in small bowl, stir until well blended.

Alternate pineapple chunks, shrimp, bacon, mushrooms, and green peppers on skewers. Brush with sauce. Broil four inches for hot coals five minutes on each side, brushing often with sauce. Yields four servings.

Aunt Stella and Adleane Spicy Fried Chicken???

???
½ C. hot sauce
Nature's Seasoning Salt
1 cup of flour

Marinate fresh parts overnight in hot sauce. Mix seasoning salt with flour in brown paper bag and put chicken in it and shake. Fry at moderate temperature until crisp and brown.

Serves four.

Mama Mary @Mary's Place #1 on menu
Southern Fried Chicken

½ C. all-purpose flour
3 T. yellow cornmeal
2 t. salt
½ t. pepper
1 fryer chicken cut up (2 ½ to 3 lbs.)
2/3 cups shortening or vegetable oil

In bag, combine flour, cornmeal, salt, and pepper. Add chicken, a few pieces at a time; shake until well coated.

In a heavy skillet over high heat, melt shortening or heat oil. Add chicken legs, thighs and back and cook until well browned on all sides, about five minutes, turning occasionally. Remove from skillet. Add chicken breast and wings and brown well on all sides, about five minutes. Return all chicken pieces to skillet and reduce heat to low. Cook uncovered 40 to 45 min., until chicken is crisp and fork-tender. Remove from skillet and drain on paper towels. Makes four servings, about 44 calories each.

Adleane and Darlene
Big Sister / Lil Sister Team
Baked Duck

1 duck
½ onion
½ apple or orange
Bacon strips (optional)

Orange juice

Salt cavity of duck. Place onion, apple, or ½ orange (peeled) inside the duck. If the duck is small, place bacon strips over the top. If the duck is fat, no bacon is needed. Place duck in a casserole, adding enough orange juice to cover about half inch of the casserole. Cover. Baste once. Bake at 350 degrees for an hour. Serve sliced very thin with orange glaze.

Mama Adleane's
Roast Leg of Lamb

Leg of Lamb
1 envelope of Lipton Onion soup mix

Rinse lamb. Place in aluminum foil. Cover lamb with onion soup on all sides. Wrap foil around lamb, sealing in tent fashion. Bake at 325 degrees until done.

Mama Adleane's
Tasty Fish Bake

¼ cup butter or margarine
2 T. minced onion
2 T. Worcestershire sauce
1 T. lemon juice
1 t. garlic salt
1 - 1 ½ lbs. fish fillets
1 T. parsley flakes
Dash paprika

Preheat oven to 425 degrees. In small saucepan, melt butter. Add onion, Worcestershire, lemon juice, and garlic salt. Arrange fish in shallow baking dish. Sprinkle with parsley and paprika. Pour sauce over fish. Bake 15 minutes. Serves four.

Mama Adleane's
Oyster Mushroom Stew

???
2 (12 oz.) cans oysters fresh or frozen
1 (10 ½ oz.) can of cream of mushroom soup
2 C. oyster liquor and milk
¼ C. butter or margarine
½ t. salt
1 T. cooking sherry
Paprika for garnish

Thaw oysters if frozen. Drain oysters and reserve liquor. Combine all ingredients except oysters and sherry in a 3-quart saucepan. Heat, stirring occasionally. Add oysters. Heat three to five minutes longer or until edges of oysters begins to curl. Add sherry. Sprinkle with paprika. Serves six.

Mama Adleane's
Broiled Trout with Cucumber

1 10-oz. packages frozen whole rainbow trout (4 trout)
¼ C. butter or margarine
¼ C. lemon juice
1 large cucumber peeled (about ½ lb.)
1 T. butter or margarine, cut into tiny pieces
2 T. minced fresh dill weed
¼ t. salt
1/8 t. pepper
Fresh dill weed sprigs

Heat broiler. Place frozen fish in an oiled 9 ½ x 13-inches. broiling pan without the rack. Melt the ¼ cup butter in a small pan over moderate heat; stir in the lemon juice. Brush the fish with half the lemon butter and broil five inches from the heat for five minutes.

Turn fish, brush with remaining butter mixture, and broil three minutes longer. While fish broils, score the cucumber lengthwise with the tines of a fork. Cut in half lengthwise and then ¼-inch-thick slices. Baste fish with pan juices and then arrange half the cucumber at each end of the pan; scatter the one tablespoon of butter over the cucumber, sprinkle minced dill weed over the fish and cucumber. Broil six to eight minutes longer or until fish is done and cucumber is crisp-tender. Sprinkle with salt and pepper; garnish with fresh dill sprigs. Makes 4 servings.

Mama Adleane's
Grandmother's
Pound Cake

1 lb. butter
1 lb. powdered sugar
6 eggs
3 C. cake flour
½ t. vanilla flavor

Grease cake pan well, or two loaf pans. Preheat oven to 350 degrees. Cream butter and sugar together. Add eggs one at a time, beating well after each egg. Blend in well sifted flour. Add vanilla. Bake at 350 degrees for ½ hour, and then reduce heat to 300 degrees for ½ hour or until cake springs back to touch. (If you like, test with a toothpick.)

Adleane's Thanksgiving Day #1 Only
Powdered Sugar Pound Cake

1½ C. butter
6 eggs
1 lb. powdered sugar
1 t. vanilla
2 ¾ C. cake flour

Cream together butter and sugar. Add eggs, one at a time. Gradually add sifted cake flour, then vanilla.

Bake in tube pan for 1 ½ hours at 300 degrees.

Mama Adleane's
Apple Pound Cake

2 C. sugar
3 C. flour
1 t. baking soda
1 t. salt
1½ C. Wesson oil
3 C. apples (cubed or chopped)
3 eggs
1 can coconut
1 can nuts

Cream oil and sugar, add flour, add 3 eggs and other ingredients. Bake for 1 hour 20 minutes at 325 degrees. Shake nuts in flour lightly this prevents nuts from settling at the bottom of cake.

Aunt Stella's Birthday Specialty
German's Chocolate Pound Cake

1 bar German's sweet chocolate
2 C. sugar
1 C. shortening
4 eggs
2 t. vanilla extract
2 t. imitation butter flavoring
1 C. buttermilk
3 C. sifted all-purpose flour
½ t. baking soda
1 t. salt

Partially melt chocolate over hot water. Remove and stir rapidly until melted. Cool. Cream sugar and shortening. Add eggs, flavorings, and buttermilk. Sift together flour baking soda, salt; add to shortening. Mix well.

Blend in chocolate. Pour into well-greased and floured 9-inch tube pan. Bake in a slow 300 degrees oven for about 1 ½ hours. Remove from pan while still hot and place under tightly fitting cover until thoroughly cooled.

Aunt Darlene's Anniversary Brown Sugar Pound Cake

1 C. vegetable shortening	½ t. salt
1 stick margarine	½ t. baking powder
1 box light brown sugar	1 C. milk
1 half cup white sugar	1 t. maple flavoring
5 eggs	1 t. vanilla flavoring
3 C. plain flour	1 C. nuts (optional)

Cream shortening and margarine with sugars. Add eggs, one at a time, beating well after each. Sift together dry ingredients and add alternately with milk. Stir in flavorings and nuts. Bake in a tube pan at 325 degrees for 1 hour and 25 minutes.

Aunt Darlene's Icing

1 stick margarine
¼ C. milk
1 C. dark brown sugar
¾ box confectioner's sugar

Combine margarine, milk, and brown sugar in boiler. Bring to a boil. Add confectioner's sugar. Spread on cake.

Mama Mary's Any Time of Year Celebration
Standard Layer Cake

1 C. butter
2 C. sugar
4 eggs, separated
3 C. flour
2 t. baking powder
1 C. milk
1 t. vanilla

Cream butter and sugar; add egg yolks, then the dry ingredients that have been sifted together, then the milk alternately. Add vanilla. Fold in stiffly beaten egg whites. Bake at 375 degrees for 30 minutes.

Mama Adleane's Mary's Place #1
Lemon Fluff Pie

3 egg yolks, well beaten
¾ C. sugar
1 T. butter
Grated rind and juice of 1 lemon
3 T. cold water
¼ C. sugar
1 9-inch baked pastry shell

Mix first five ingredients in top of double boiler. Cook in double boiler until thick and add ¼ cup sugar.

Pour mixture into baked 9-inch pastry shell and brown quickly under the broiler unit of range.

Mama Adleane's
Homemade Ice Cream

1 can condensed milk (Eagle brand) large
1 can evaporated milk (large)
6-10 eggs
¾ C. sugar
1 quart milk
Pinch salt
Vanilla, rum, brandy, etc. flavoring or fruit

Mix first four ingredients; pour into churn. Add milk to within four or five inches from top. Churn until firm.

We give God all glory. Amen.

Printed in the United States
By Bookmasters